Find Your
Voice

JOANNA CROSSE

Find Your
Voice

How clear communication
can transform your life

piatkus

PIATKUS

First published in Great Britain in 2009 by Piatkus

A CIP catalogue record for this book
is available from the British Library

ISBN 978-0-7499-4177-2

Typeset in Warnock Pro by Phoenix Photosetting Ltd
Printed and bound in Great Britain by MPG Books, Bodmin, Cornwall

Papers used by Piatkus are natural, renewable and recyclable
products sourced from well-managed forests and certified
in accordance with the rules of the Forest Stewardship Council.

Mixed Sources
Product group from well-managed
forests and other controlled sources
www.fsc.org Cert no. SGS-COC-004081
© 1996 Forest Stewardship Council

Piatkus
An imprint of
Little, Brown Book Group
100 Victoria Embankment
London EC4Y 0DY

An Hachette UK Company
www.hachette.co.uk

www.piatkus.co.uk

To everyone who has helped me to find my voice and, in turn, co-created this book.

Contents

Acknowledgements

S pecial thanks to my children, Skye, Merrick and Sedona, who in their own unique ways have helped me to speak my truth. A big thank you to everyone who has contributed to *Find Your Voice* – experts and clients alike. Many thanks to my agent Susan Mears for her support and encouragement, to commissioning editor Helen Stanton and to Jan Cutler – editor extraordinaire!

Introduction

I am delighted to write this book, which is all about helping you to find your voice. This is not just about the voice in a physical sense but about how you speak your personal truth. This means finding your authentic voice and being able to communicate with integrity, whether it is to family, friends or a large audience. I'll also be describing how you can find your personal voice, which is about expressing your uniqueness. This book is aimed at helping you find the confidence to do just that and to speak up and be heard.

I have rarely met a person who doesn't have concerns about how they sound, and yet it is often an aspect of ourselves that we neglect or choose to ignore, because we feel uncomfortable about it. Our voice is not just a sound box, but an intimate and intricate part of who we are, and it's a reflection of our unique personality. After many years of finding my voice and helping hundreds of others to find theirs, I want to pass on the simple tools that will help you to build up your confidence and encourage you to use your voice to its full potential. The book is also a guide to help you communicate clearly and effectively in any situation, from the workplace to your home life – and if you want to promote yourself through the media.

I have spent more than three decades working in the media, as a newspaper journalist, and newsreader and presenter on regional and national radio and television, and I have coached many other broadcast professionals and individuals in the corporate, public and private sectors. As a published author, I have also been on the other side of the microphone, being interviewed, so I fully understand any fears that people have about how they might present themselves in a professional situation. I have used these experiences to cover a wide range of scenarios where we use our voice, to help you to be fully prepared to use yours.

On a personal level, I have been in recovery from addiction for many years, and through this I have developed a great interest in personal development and helping people to find their voice through even the most challenging of times. I am also a single parent of three teenagers, so I have plenty of life experience to draw on! The book gives you ideas on communication and finding your voice in personal situations as well as in the workplace. I use my experience, and that of others, to illustrate how you can find your true voice so that your message is received clearly.

FINDING YOUR VOICE

I have been interested in the whole subject of voice since I was a child. I remember being asked to do readings at school assemblies and thinking how good it would be if I could have a job like that when I grew up! Experience has shown me that we are born with particular gifts, and we set off on a path to fulfil those desires that can seem very long and winding at times; ultimately, though, it leads us to a greater understanding of ourselves and helps us to live our lives in a more meaningful way. Your voice is an external symbol of who you are and what is going on inside you, and finding your voice in the truest sense of the word is about achieving your potential in the work you want to do and the relationships you have with friends, family and colleagues.

Find Your Voice sets out to help you communicate more effectively in every area of your life. It also covers learning to be assertive, how to speak up in situations that frighten you, and how to find a clear way to talk to other people and in different situations, whether it's with a child or the chief executive of a company, at a job interview or in a broadcast.

I'm going to dispel the fears and the myths surrounding the whole subject of the voice. The truth of the matter is that finding *your* voice and being able to use it effectively in any situation takes confidence and courage, and I'm going to be taking you through some simple steps to achieve just that.

Our voice is an expression of who we are, and this book will look at practical ways to improve it and the message we want to deliver. It's not just about how you sound, it's much more about who you are, what you want to say and how you can be truly heard. If I could put the success of my training and coaching sessions down to one factor, then it would be helping others to build confidence. I often say that I work from the inside out: when I have helped people understand themselves better and overcome some of their inner fears, it is reflected on the outside.

The overall aim of this book is to give you some comprehensive and practical advice about how to use your voice and improve your communication. It's not just what we say, but how we say it. Above all else, it's not about trying to be, or to sound like, somebody else, but improving your voice and the message you want to deliver. Good communication is also about learning how to be a good listener.

I have been inspired by the people I have trained and met, some of whom have overcome many odds to find their true voices, so I have included some of their stories and experiences in the book. I hope these will encourage you to put aside any fears you may have about your voice and how you present yourself, and that you will become more confident on the inside and the outside.

I suggest that you read through the book, but it is also intended to be a useful handbook, where you can refer back to relevant chapters depending on whatever is appropriate for you at any given time.

The book is divided into ten chapters, covering:

VOICE

Our voice is an instrument that is an expression of who we are. In this chapter we look at how you can find the confidence to use your voice to its full potential. We look at the power of words and language and some research about the voice, as well as practical exercises and some tips from people who work in broadcasting.

YOUR PERSONAL VOICE

Finding your personal voice is just as important as finding your voice for speaking in the public or the business arena. Who we are and what we do to make our lives more purposeful and meaningful is critical to finding our voice.

CLEAR COMMUNICATION

Everyone wants to be heard and to have their say, but how often do we feel that nobody is listening to us and that our message is misunderstood? In this chapter we look at how to get our message across and listen well. And there is the whole subject of non-verbal communication and our body language, which have a large role to play in the way we express ourselves. Also included are some inspirational stories from people who have to communicate differently from others.

ASSERTIVENESS SKILLS

Being able to speak confidently and clearly, getting your message across as intended and being heard are qualities of assertiveness. In this chapter you will discover how to avoid being aggressive or passive and learn how to say what you want to say and to be heard.

PRESENTATION SKILLS

Putting on a great show is all about the preparation. If you don't prepare, you prepare to fail. So this chapter is about considering your audience, targeting your message and then acting naturally in your delivery to keep them listening from start to finish. I hope this will inspire you to capitalise on your own talents and give your best possible performance.

INTERVIEW SKILLS

This chapter suggests ways to help you be at your best in an interview situation, whether for a place at university, a new job or an internal promotion, or if you are facing redundancy and having to start all over again. It focuses on discovering how good you are, what you have to offer and allowing what's unique about you to come through. There is also a section on how to be interviewed in the media.

RAISING YOUR PROFILE

In this chapter we explore the importance of reviewing your own curriculum vitae – not just by keeping it up to date but also by reminding yourself of your qualities and experience, which can be assets for any potential employer. Although many of us dislike the idea of promoting ourselves, this section looks at the art of internal and external networking in a way that you can feel comfortable with. There are also tips on how to use the media and PR effectively to get your message across.

YOUR BODY, YOUR VOICE

Our minds and bodies work together, and in this chapter I look at how caring about our bodies ultimately affects what we have to say and how we say it. It's all part of our life's journey that makes each one of us unique. Dealing with stress and living a healthy lifestyle helps us to feel well and confident – which benefits our voice.

CHILDREN AND YOUNG ADULTS

This chapter explores our relationship with children as part of our life's journey and how it affects our personal voice. I also cover communicating effectively with them and helping them to find their own voice. I have included inspiring stories from parents, teachers and a foster carer, who prove that helping young people discover their unique voice can be life changing.

A CONTINUING JOURNEY OF DISCOVERY

This book wouldn't have been complete without stories from individuals from all walks of life who have, in their own unique ways, found their voice or helped others to find theirs. Finding your voice is not just about how we can improve our communication skills and vocal delivery but also about how we can fulfil our potential and lead a meaningful life, as these stories illustrate.

I hope that through this book you will discover new ways to communicate with confidence and that you will enjoy the journey as you find *your* voice.

Joanna Crosse

1
Voice

Your voice is an expression of who you are. What you say and how you say it has a resonance that speaks volumes. Your voice is like a musical instrument, but however fine it may be, if you don't learn to play it well you're never going to get the best sound from it. In this chapter we are going to look at how you can use your voice to its full potential and overcome any insecurities you may have about how you sound (or how you think you sound). Having the confidence to find all the notes in your voice is something that will help you promote yourself in both your personal and professional life.

WHAT DOES YOUR VOICE SAY ABOUT YOU?

Scientists across the world have deduced that our voice says much about who we are and this reinforces the concept that human beings have a deep longing to be heard and a strong desire to find their vocal expression in the world.

I am fascinated by voices, because each one is unique and says so much about a person, in much the same way as a signature reveals aspects of an individual's character. How your voice sounds shows others how you feel. When you hear a dull, flat voice, what does it suggest to you? Does it seem that they could be someone who lacks energy, vitality or confidence? If they sound dull and flat it could be because that is how they feel about themselves or their life. How do you feel about a person who talks in a whisper? Do you feel perhaps that they don't really want to be heard? This could be a sign that they are not confident about themselves or their voice. How do you react to a strident or harsh voice? Do you feel that the speaker is aggressive or opinionated?

When we hear someone speak we create an impression of that person from the way their voice sounds to us.

The way we sound to ourselves and others

Although we all have an impression of others' voices, most of us have little idea how we sound ourselves, until we hear our voice played back from a recording, and we are usually very surprised. Our own voice often sounds unrecognisable to us, and I have never met anyone who has not felt uncomfortable hearing their voice for the first time. So, before we can feel comfortable about our speaking voice we have to become used to hearing it. Because we don't normally hear ourselves we are usually oblivious to the fact that we may sound rude or loud or soft, for example. Sounding aggressive (rude) or passive (soft) is often a sign of insecurity, and later in the book I'll be explaining how our true self is reflected in our voice. People can tell a great deal about others just by listening to how they talk.

Our voices paint a picture of ourselves

There have been a number of studies into the voice and its effect on the listener. Some recent research carried out by

Sheffield University revealed that the 'perfect voice' could be created by a formula based on the combination of tone, speed, frequency, the number of words per minute and intonation. Vocal traits that are associated with positive characteristics, such as confidence and trust – a reassuring tone and a confident, believable quality – scored highly with listeners. Other studies have shown that the voice provides information about ourselves to others. Apart from your gender and age, your voice conveys your true emotions even when you try to withhold them. Studies have shown that you can even tell if someone is lying to you by the change in their voice's pitch or tone.

Participants in the research concluded that they could judge someone's personality purely by their voice. They found that a louder and faster voice was a sign of an extrovert, whereas a softer and slower voice would be that of the introvert. Another study by Stanford University found that people could even recognise personality in voices that were computer generated.

In fact, research has shown that because your voice encapsulates so much information, it affects how others perceive you as much as, or even more than, your physical appearance.

If your voice is your 'signature tune' then how you say something will reveal a great deal about you.

An attractive voice means an attractive person?

Some research has revealed that people with attractive voices are usually perceived as having more desirable personality characteristics. This is known as the 'vocal attractiveness stereotype'. I think all this research certainly proves that your voice matters.

Being heard – the right way

We often spend time and money making ourselves look good, but how often do we consider the impact that we make on others when we open our mouth? Our voice is such an intimate part of ourselves, but it is often difficult to find the correct words and the right way to represent who we really are; for example, how many times have you felt unheard or misunderstood? This is because it is not just what you say but it is also the way you say it and how you sound that are important.

How do others create their impression of us? Well, visual impact plays the largest role, but 38 per cent of our success depends on how we sound. In situations where people cannot see you, however, the importance of the sound of your voice is judged as 83 per cent. As a voice coach I have found that people frequently pay little attention to their voice, even though they have concerns about the way they present themselves when speaking. And if they are lacking confidence they will try to avoid giving presentations or speaking to large groups.

In my experience, however, nobody's voice is ever as bad as they think it is, but it often needs developing and coaching. A voice that is not used to its full potential is like owning a wonderful instrument that you keep locked away in a music case and have never used. You're wasting something wonderful if you don't learn how to use your voice, and the way to release that potential is to find confidence.

Although we are going to look at how to make the best possible use of your voice in terms of presentations, we are actually always presenting ourselves in one form or another to other people, whether it is to an individual or a group. Finding your voice is important whatever situation you are in.

PRESENTATIONS: ACT NATURALLY

There is a very simple and easy way to use your voice properly when you have to give a presentation or speech, and that is to act naturally. It is essential to be yourself so that you can bring spontaneous expression to what you are saying rather than going into a 'presenter mode'. When we have conversations with people we don't usually think about how we are speaking – we are just being naturally expressive. In my coaching sessions when people are struggling to sound natural I remind them that in a normal conversation they would not be worrying about whether they should sound sad, happy or enthusiastic. This is because they would be connected to what they are saying and giving the words their natural meaning.

When you're giving a presentation it's easy to wander off mentally, but if you are not connected to what you are saying you are not engaging with your own words. How, then, can you expect the person who is listening to be interested in what you have to say? If you are switched off from what you are saying, you cannot expect the listener to be switched on.

Just be yourself

Being yourself is the key to improving your voice and getting your message across. We will be exploring the whole subject of preparation and the messages we put out, but we first need to be clear that one of the foundation stones to a more resonant and believable delivery is simply to be yourself. This helps you to come across more naturally and in a more authentic way.

Case Study: Sameena

Sameena is a television presenter and although she has a great deal of broadcasting experience she had a tendency to be stilted when talking on air.

'Be yourself – two words that have rung loud and clear ever since I began presenting ten years ago, but why couldn't I get it right? What did it mean and why was it that as soon as I heard the words "cue Sam" I seemed to stop being myself? Well, experience is a valuable tool, and you hope you get better with practice, but it wasn't until seven years into my presenting career after training with Jo that I finally began to understand what being myself actually meant. Her approach involved assessing my personality and the situation surrounding my presentation – in other words dealing with the root cause of any issues before tackling the faults themselves. It was after talking things through and watching tapes of previous on-screen performances that I was able to identify my own shortcomings and, more importantly, recognise why they were happening. Presenting live after the training session felt so much better and, not surprisingly, everyone noticed. I finally understood that being myself was about being comfortable with who I am and not being afraid to show that – particularly on screen.'

SOUND

The ancient mystics were aware that we could heal our body, mind and emotions through the power of sound, and they did this through music and singing. In modern times we have helped all kinds of behavioural issues through the benefits of music therapy, or through working with tuning forks or by singing mantras. There is no question that sound and its power are fundamental to our lives. Quantum physicists and mystics alike share the view that everything in the universe is made up of vibrational frequencies.

Sound is amazingly powerful: the human voice is capable of shattering a glass at a certain frequency, and scientists have also proved through experiments that sound waves can shape different materials.

There are numerous studies into the power of sound and its ability to heal, but in the context of the voice it is how someone's delivery can make us feel. I know that some voices can keep my attention, whereas others don't, and when I listen to a wonderful, rich resonant voice it can feel very therapeutic. In basic terms, if someone says something loving and kind to you in a gentle tone of voice it's likely to make you feel good, but if someone yells at you in a harsh and strident way then it's going to have a destructive effect.

THE POWER OF THOUGHT

If you have ever believed that your thoughts don't influence your life, think again. The mind is continually attracting thoughts, influences and circumstances that reflect our own particular thinking and way of being. Although the concept of mind power is not new, it has come back into vogue in recent years. We hear phrases such as 'like attracts like', 'what a man thinketh upon, that he becomes'. Thoughts – whether positive or negative – can become habit forming. If you dwell on the same repetitive thought, it will create a groove, and eventually you will be thinking the same old thought without even being aware of it.

Thoughts are, like everything else, on a wave or frequency, and there is scientific evidence to suggest that what we think about is drawn to ourselves like a magnet. The power of positive thinking has been used by the medical profession to encourage patients to visualise themselves getting better, and there has been a great deal of evidence over the years that suggests we can do this.

Tuning into now

We have millions of thoughts that constantly race around our heads, but many of these are our 'inner critic': our self-doubt and the part of us that puts a negative spin on what we are trying to achieve. Unfortunately, our thoughts don't necessarily stop when we have something important to say, and this can get in the way of what we are saying. It is especially destructive if we are speaking publicly. So, to speak effectively in a way that comes across as confident and interesting we must completely tune into the present moment and think only about what is happening *now*. This will bring clarity, focus and power to what we have say. Most importantly, we must tune out our inner critic, because it will try to distract us from our message.

The inner critic

Our inner world can often be governed by the loud voice of our ego, which drowns out our intuitive voice and the natural instincts we are born with. This loud voice is our inner critic. When I first explain this to the people I work with they are usually visibly relieved to know that they are not the only person living with a voice that often contradicts their own gut feelings. However, although we might be convinced by the destructive thoughts generated by our ego, it's important to understand that even though they may be believable and convincing they are not necessarily true. This is because the inner critic may be hanging on to old messages that we could have picked up in our childhood or from a negative past relationship; for example, when you were a child your parents may have told you that you were lazy and would never achieve anything. This might stop you from working hard to achieve, because you are convinced you will fail. We are all inclined to hold on to negative messages from the past and apply them to our daily lives. If you tell somebody enough times that they are no good, they will eventually believe it.

....

Exercise: recognising your own inner critic

1 We're so used to living with the voice of the inner critic that we don't realise it's there until we stop and listen to it. Think about any negative personality traits you believe you have or about the skills you believe you don't have, or can't do very well.

2 Why do you think these things about yourself? Is it because someone has said something to you in the past; for example, if you've always believed you couldn't draw, think back to when you were a small child. Did a teacher, parent or someone you were at school with say something about your drawing? Have you every really tried to draw? Does the feeling that you don't have any ability stop you from trying, even though you might enjoy it? This is the inner critic holding you back by repeating the message so often that you become convinced by it.

3 When you look at yourself in the mirror, are you accepting of your appearance or do you find that there are parts you really don't like? Perhaps you feel you're fat. If other people tell you that you aren't, does this make any difference to the way you see your body? Why do you think you feel this way? Is it because you compare yourself with celebrities? Your inner critic will try to keep you small by constantly comparing you to these unrealistic stereotypes and making you feel inadequate.

4 Recognise that the inner critic is working to undermine you, and think about the negative labels you give yourself. It's the human condition to feel we're not good enough, but we have to work on overcoming these beliefs because they can stop us from doing things in life.

5 Now, consciously try to block the negative messages you are receiving from within and try to overcome them; for example, we can try new things in life. We may find we're good at them, or we may find that we can enjoy taking part and only being passable at them. When it comes to our personal appearance, we can learn to be more comfortable with the way we are, and understand that there are many ways to be attractive. Remember also that when we compare ourselves to celebrities, the pictures we see are significantly airbrushed and 'corrected' by computer, so they are not of 'real' people.

6 When we banish the inner critic we raise awareness about ourselves and this makes us stronger and more confident.

Our intuition

I have to come realise that the most powerful part of my work with people is helping them manage their own inner critic. It is this voice that keeps us small and too scared to take that leap, because we are frightened we will not make it to the other side. The intuitive voice, however, is that deep inner knowing; the very first response we might have to a situation. Whenever I have ignored my intuitive hunch I have regretted it. Recently, a person asked me to meet him under the pretext of a potential work opportunity. I did turn up for the meeting but felt very uncomfortable in his presence and was suspicious about his motives from the outset. In other words,

I was on my guard – and that was a good thing as it turned out, because he didn't offer me any work opportunities but instead tried to manipulate and flatter me into a pyramid-selling scheme. I haven't become cynical over the years but hopefully I have become wiser and much more tuned into my intuition. This is the signpost to follow, and it will lead us to our personal voice.

PHYSICAL PROBLEMS

Sometimes we feel physically unable to speak from the heart. Think of some of the phrases that we might use to describe those times when we can't actually express ourselves; such as when we 'feel choked', or when words are 'stuck' in our throat, when we speak 'through gritted teeth' or we cope with a difficult situation by adopting the 'stiff upper lip'. Being stuck in this way means that you are unable to say what you want to.

Speaking 'through gritted teeth' suggests anger, and a 'stiff upper lip' will hold back our pain and sadness. The phrase 'feeling choked' is when people feel gagged and unable to speak properly. Interestingly, though, it's not necessarily others that are stopping us from speaking, but we can project our own inner fears and anxieties onto those around us, so that although it feels as if they are gagging us it's really that we feel we can't speak out.

In this book you will find stories from people who have had to break through their own personal barriers to find their voice. A victim of an abusive relationship once told me that ultimately it is only the victim who can find the power to leave. In other words, when you stand up for yourself either verbally or metaphorically by physically leaving, you are then finding your inner confidence, courage and belief to change the situation. This inner confidence is your 'personal voice', and I'll be explaining about this in the next chapter.

I have found that there is a direct correlation between the sound of someone's voice and what is going on psychologically or emotionally for them. Perhaps they are not able to get the words out, speaking in hushed tones – almost as if they fear being heard.

Speech impediments

If you have a speech impediment, such as a stammer, this will make using your voice to its full potential a real challenge. However, it *is* possible, and I have met people who have overcome the most extraordinary vocal problems – some of whom have eventually worked in broadcasting.

Delete the problem!

I remember working with a group of people from the media who were used to working on the technical side, but were on a course to learn to be broadcasters. One of that group was a guy who had a stammer – or so he believed:

Case Study: Giles

At the beginning of our session I asked Giles to tell me about himself. He chatted away about his family and upbringing, then suddenly he came to a grinding halt. He hesitated and could not get the words out. I could almost hear his inner critical voice urging him to tell me about his stammer; in other words, he didn't start to stammer until he reminded himself that he had one. When I pointed this out to him he looked surprised, and I then suggested that he try imagining the stammer was an unwanted computer program that he could just delete. As the session progressed, I got him to record a news bulletin. Again, he started off perfectly confidently with no hint of hesitation, then that inner critic kicked in again ready to sabotage his delivery. 'I can't,' he said.

'You can,' I said.

'I can't.'

'Yes, you can! You've just been reading that bulletin without any problems. Keep going!'

And he did, word-perfectly. Afterwards, he admitted that he had been going to a speech therapist for several years. I offered an alternative viewpoint. Perhaps he had a stammer because he *believed* he did.

Think of the word 'imagine'. It means to 'image in'. This is what was happening to Giles.

Finding the right image

We can all 'image in' anything we choose; that is, we can believe any image of ourselves. I am not discounting the fact that our fears and concerns do become manifest on a physical level, but I have worked with countless people who have overcome some quite severe physical speech problems by dealing with their pesky inner critic. Here's an example: you know the situation that you have been dreading, and the nervous build-up to it you have been experiencing? That is an example of making your fears become reality. If you give something enough attention, you are literally imaging it into your reality. However, you can just as easily replace that negative image with a more positive one.

Case Study: Gemma

Gemma was extremely nervous about giving a talk to a group of students, even though it was on a subject she knew a great deal about. Over the phone she told me that when she had to give any kind of presentation she found she lost her voice or it had become like a whisper. Before she even arrived for our session I was confident that I could help her sort this out. The key was unlocking the psychological block and, as it turned out, she had a traumatic personal situation to deal with that was taking up a great deal of energy and thought. When I helped her to replace the very negative picture she had in her mind with a positive one, it helped to release the constriction in her throat so that she could find her true voice. It was as if there had been a hand around her throat squeezing the life force – and her voice – out of her.

OPENING THE DOOR THROUGH SELF-CONFIDENCE

Using your voice well and to the best of your ability is about self-confidence. I visited a youth-based Internet radio project called Spark Radio in Wiltshire, which is run by young volunteers who give out information and advice to youngsters in their area. It is run by the station manager, Jamie Flukes, who explains why this innovative project is such a good example of how a group of people have built up their self-confidence and found their voice – and been heard:

It has given my young presenters a voice over the air. In some cases it's just playing their music tastes to a wider audience, but for others it's a real chance to talk about issues and things that concern them and to get themselves heard.

One of my presenters is homeless, and yet he never misses a show; another one of my young people is living in a children's home, yet she also never misses a show. In some cases it's physical issues that my presenters have to cope with. I have a presenter on the station who is excluded from school and has a history of being in trouble, but he found his voice through radio and it is turning his life around. He never misses his show and has become a valued member of the team. In each case Spark means something different to each, but also collectively it is something to be proud of and to shape, and ultimately it is their soapbox and their opportunity to get their voices heard.

I went along to the radio station to talk to one of the presenters, Dan McAleavy, who is 20 years old and has cerebral palsy, which affects his legs and an arm. I sat with Dan while he presented his one-hour show and, as it turned out, I was the one being interviewed rather than the other way round! What really impressed me was his natural confidence and broadcast ability, despite having extra problems to deal with. He used his voice well and was not frightened to let his delivery breathe – an example of a true performer. For Dan, being able to broadcast has greatly boosted his self-esteem:

Case Study: Dan

'At first I was very nervous, but now I don't feel nervous, so it's really helped to improve my confidence. Someone was there to help me with the technical aspects, as I am not very technically adept ... I had a youth worker who was really good; she had the same sense of humour as me and we had a ball, making up comedy features for my programme. Spark Radio has enabled me to release the comedy element in my personality. My head is full of all sorts of ridiculous comedy notions and I have been able to express these through being on the radio. Being a broadcaster has improved my reading and research skills too.'

I think this story proves that we all have a voice that should be heard, and the only thing that can really stop us getting out there and using it to its full potential is a lack of confidence. One of my favourite mantras in my voice-coaching sessions is that finding your voice is all about making progress, not expecting perfection.

FINDING YOUR PHYSICAL VOICE

We can speak up for ourselves and give voice to our opinions. We can also choose how we use our voice. Will it emanate as harmonious notes or will it sound flat, dull and uninteresting? Try this visualisation:

Exercise: story visualisation

1 Whatever situation you are in, imagine you are telling one person a story. Use this visualisation whether you are on the telephone, delivering a presentation to hundreds, chairing a business meeting or talking to one individual.

2 It's important to make sure that every person listening to your words feels as if you are talking to them alone.

3 Get them hooked in and they will be hanging on to your every word.

The richness of colours

One of the most effective exercises I have given people over the years is asking them to imagine their voice as a palette of paint colours. The story they are telling is the picture they are painting, and using colours will give it richness. Whether I am training jockeys, health professionals or television presenters, this idea has a resonance with them all, and it works because it is simple.

In a moment I will ask you to imagine your voice is a palette of paint colours. Day to day, we probably use only about five out of a possible 25 colours, but when we have to give a presentation or performance of any kind we need to give the picture more colour and vibrancy to ensure the listener hears what we are saying. Somebody once told me that in broadcast terms the microphone or camera takes away about 50 per cent of a voice's impact, so we have to boost what we are saying without losing the naturalness. So, when it comes to a presentation of any kind, it's important to use the full range of colours in our palette. If you only use a few pastel shades, the picture on your canvas will be limited and will not say very much. Use the full range of colours, however, and your audience will receive a more vivid picture with greater feeling and meaning. It's as if the extra colours add depth, perspective and vibrancy to what you are saying.

Remember to focus

The other important aspect in using your voice is to focus fully on what you're saying. If you are not engaged, your listeners cannot be engaged either, so it is important to focus your attention in the right place. It's like the difference between going for a jog and running a race to win it. If you're jogging in the park it's OK to enjoy the scenery and notice people watching as you're jogging along, but if you are on that starting block waiting to run your race and win it, you would not allow yourself to be distracted by looking at the crowds. It's all about focus and being present in the moment.

Focus is essentially the difference between reading a few pages of a book and not remembering a word you have read, or being totally engaged and absorbed by the content, reacting to everything you are reading. Focus is essential to bring you into the present moment.

So, how do you find those extra colours to add richness to your voice and focus yourself to become present? This simple exercise will get you into the zone:

....

Exercise: your paint palette

1 Start by taking a few deep breaths. Breathe out the tension in your body and concentrate on your breathing. Ignore the little voice in your head that's trying to distract you.

2 Put your feet flat on the floor. Imagine you have roots going deep into the ground. This will help you to feel centred and grounded. Continue to concentrate on regular breathing. As you sink into this more relaxed breathing pattern you will start to feel more centred and grounded.

3 Imagine that all the colours in your paint palette are in your stomach. You are going to use your voice from that part of your body rather than from the top part of your body – the chest area or above – which would lead to a high, disconnected sound.

4 Try speaking an octave lower. Count down 'three–two–one', and with each number go down in pitch. This will help you to find the extra colours in your palette. By starting lower you will use much more of your voice, so you will not only sound better but you will also feel better, because being centred will help you to feel connected.

5 Now bring yourself fully into present time and start to find your true voice.

....

GETTING INTO FOCUS

🔊 Remember to breathe.

🔊 Root your feet.

🔊 Tune into the present.

🔊 Tune out the inner critic.

🔊 When you speak, start lower and slower to help you manage the message rather than letting the message manage you.

WORDS AND LANGUAGE

The way we say something is critical, but there is also no question that words have power in themselves.

Fact Some extraordinary research was begun about ten years ago by the Japanese scientist Dr Masaru Emoto, who discovered that molecules of water are affected by our thoughts, words and feelings. He produced photographs that illustrate how, when water is frozen, the crystals reveal the concentrated thoughts that had been directed towards the water when it was liquid. Dr Emoto believes that words are an expression of the soul and that the condition of our soul is likely to have a large impact on the water that makes up as much as 70 per cent of our body. Bad words negatively affect the structure of water whereas good words help the water crystals take beautiful shapes. Interestingly, Dr Emoto says that in

all his research the most beautiful crystal formation of them all for him is the one created by the words 'love and gratitude'.

The language we use and the words we choose are vitally important. As words have power and energy we need to be discerning about how we use them. Have you ever felt that someone's words melt your heart or pierce you like an arrow? Behind the words is an energetic impact that can leave a dent on a physical level. That is why there are so many phrases like 'broken heart', 'shattered dreams', 'cut like a knife'.

When I was making a documentary about domestic violence, every person I interviewed, without exception, both men and women, said that the most damaging part of the abuse was the psychological and verbal insults they had received. However catastrophic the physical abuse, the lasting scars came from the unkind and demeaning words that had been hurled at them. Words and language have tremendous power, as does the intent behind them.

There's more to communication than words

One student I worked with, who was learning two languages for her degree, said that living in different cultures had taught her that language was so much more than just words. She said she had come to see that language was only a small percentage of communication. She had stopped being concerned about understanding every single word that people spoke to her, as she realised that the context of the conversation as well as the gestures, tone and facial expressions are things that are consistent between languages and cultures; they are just as helpful in understanding and communicating with people as the words that are used.

When you are lost for words

Sometimes you find yourself in an unfamiliar situation and are completely lost for words, but by building up confidence you will be able to speak in any situation. Lawrence Galkoff is a broadcast professional who has worked across the whole range of television and radio for the past 25 years. As a sound specialist and trainer he has come across many people who find it hard to find their voice when they're not behind the microphone.

Practice will help with confidence, and that is so important in making your voice heard. I knew one presenter who had a regular daily show on a national radio station. He went to the building society to apply for a mortgage, and although he was brilliant behind a microphone where he was in his comfort zone, he could not talk to individuals where he didn't feel in control. He stuttered his way through the interview and the building society turned down his application, as they didn't believe that he worked as a DJ.

Another presenter, who has presented the biggest shows on national radio to millions of listeners a day, would hide so that he couldn't be seen by people he didn't know. Again, he was great in his comfort zone but shy in front of strangers. So, build up your confidence and feel comfortable speaking to people. Your opinion and knowledge is as valuable as anyone else's and you have as much right to be heard as anyone else.

HOW YOU USE YOUR VOICE

This leads to the whole subject of pace, pause, tone and pitch. Although we do need to work on those elements so that they become natural, I always emphasise to people I am coaching not to get caught in the trap of worrying about pace, tone, pitch and pause when speaking, because they will become a major distraction. If, while you are speaking, you and your inner critic start to debate how good you are sounding or not, or what tone of voice you should be using, or how fast or slow you should be, you will completely disengage from the script or the point of the story. What happens then is that you create a sing-song delivery. In other words you will be trying to input colour into your story without connecting with the content. That means you create a rhythmic up-and-down pattern that bears no relation to the words and holds no true reflection or meaning to what you are saying. Instead, get out of your head and into the content. Be interested and you will sound interesting and engaging.

Reading to children

One of the best ways to practise any kind of vocal delivery is to read to children. Firstly, they will demand you become involved with the story, and secondly, they will not be polite enough to look interested when they are not. Children can be the harshest critics, and they are the first to let you know if they are bored or uninterested. So, reading a story with lots of enthusiasm and colour, and painting a vivid picture, is just what children want. And somehow it is less embarrassing to engage fully in front of a child than an adult. Remember that the more you work at being interested in your delivery the easier it will become.

Sounding natural and being a great storyteller does take practice. But practise being more of yourself rather than trying to impersonate someone else.

Talk to people, not yourself

It is also important to work at improving your voice and delivery in front of real people. You can exacerbate bad habits or even create negative speech patterns if you stand in front of the mirror with a hairbrush or start reading aloud to yourself vast column inches of a newspaper. This will not help you engage with an audience, whose reaction would most definitely give you feedback. Talking in front of real people will accelerate your performance improvement and help you to develop your voice.

Pace and pause

One of the many bad habits people develop is to speak quickly without ever pausing properly. This happens particularly when people are nervous, where there is a tendency to rush your words and not pause for breath. When you do this you can easily lose the thread of your message and drift away from the present moment. This happens because instead of thinking about what you are actually saying right now you are scanning ahead of yourself and possibly worrying about another part of your talk.

Rushing words this way is a psychological issue. It's almost as if we feel that if we rush it we will get our speech, presentation, or whatever we are delivering, out of the way as quickly as possible. The problem with this is that not only will you disconnect from what you are saying but so will your audience. They will simply not be able to keep up with you, because you will not be giving them any time to assimilate or digest the information you have given them. Let your delivery breathe, and give the viewer some catch-up time.

When speaking, less is definitely more, because if you fill every available space with a word, everything will merge into one. To use your voice well you must incorporate silence and breath, which act like paragraphs. Remember that every time you take a breath you will feel and sound better, and your audience will be able to hear what you are saying and react to the information they are being given. If you talk too quickly, they will simply be wondering about something you said earlier and not keeping up with you.

Tone

Words are meaningless until we inject meaning into them. Tone is the feeling or emotion you put into your voice, which then affects how the words actually sound to someone else. We can only add feeling by talking at a pace where we are thinking about what we are saying and are thoroughly connected to the content. This way we will naturally give the words the tone they deserve. As I have mentioned many times before, being in the present is all important for every aspect of using your voice, because you are then involved with the words you are saying, as you are saying them.

Pitch

When we talk about pitch we are describing the patterns of stress and intonation in our voice. The problem with thinking about this while we're speaking is that the minute a person starts to worry about how they sound their voice falls into a false pattern, which is a repetitive and rather monotonous rhythm that underlines what they're saying. The perfect pitch is when we are thinking about what we're saying and bringing natural expression to our words.

VOICE TIPS

🔊 Imagine your voice is a palette of colours – use as many as you can so that your picture is more vivid.

🔊 Breathe and root your feet.

🔊 If you tense up, so will your voice, so keep relaxed.

🔊 Start lower and slower.

🔊 Be yourself and imagine you're just talking to one person.

🔊 Don't let self-doubt get in the way of your performance.

🔊 Stay present and connected to every word.

THE EVER-CHANGING VOICE

I encourage all speakers to act naturally, but this also means we should accept that our voices change over the years. Finding our voice means embracing these changes and making them work for us.

Jenni Mills, who is an author and voice coach, says it took her a long time as a broadcaster to find her own voice, and she offers some comforting advice to younger people starting out:

Something I understand now, after a couple of decades as a voice coach, is the comforting fact that voices mature. Men's voices, of course, break and deepen dramatically in adolescence, as a result of hormones and physiology, but women's voices also become richer and lower pitched, though the change is often later, in their mid-twenties. It was certainly true of mine . . . and I've heard the same phenomenon in so many of the female broadcasters I've trained since then that I could easily believe this is a physiological phenomenon, less marked but similar to boys' voices breaking. After all, our bodies go on changing in subtle ways through each decade and these factors can affect the timbre of your voice. On the other hand, the personality grows too, so perhaps it's equally to do with life experiences . . . no one actively wants to court bad experiences, but they can be a foundation to build on, and you can learn more about yourself in the process.

Throughout my life, experiences have changed me and had an impact on how I sound and, perhaps more importantly, on what I say. A rich and resonant voice encapsulates wisdom, maturity and authenticity. As our handwriting and physique changes and matures while we grow, so too does our voice. Expect and welcome those changes, and go with them.

In Chapter 2 I will explain how important it is to find your own personal voice – the voice that expresses those characteristics that make you unique. It's this aspect that will enrich what you have to say, and it develops through the experiences we encounter on life's journey.

2

Discover Your Personal Voice

I n Chapter 1 I explained how people create an impression of us through the way we sound and that when we are speaking we have to be ourselves and tune into the moment. When we gain self-belief we are able to speak with confidence and feel relaxed about ourselves, regardless of how many people we are speaking to. Having this feeling comes through discovering our own personal voice through our lifelong journey of experiences.

Finding your own personal voice means figuring out what makes you individual and unique; it's key to being confident about talking to others or using your voice in public.

There is a quote that I particularly like, because it's saying that it's OK to be yourself and that you should listen to your intuition and be guided by your inner knowing rather than being overly influenced by the outside:

'Be yourself. This is something you can do better than any other. Listen to the inward voice and bravely obey that.'
(unknown)

Finding your voice in a practical way is tied up with your confidence levels and sense of self-worth. Let's now look at the importance of finding the real you.

WHAT'S HAPPENED TO OUR INDIVIDUALITY?

We seem to admire those who dare to flaunt their individuality, and yet fashion, music, culture and cuisine is all about passing fads and creating followers. Let's look at the clothes we wear: over the years the same stores have become commonplace in every high street, and even in major cities across the world, and although we may not feel we all dress the same, when we buy our clothes from these shops we are being robbed of our individuality. So, what is it that stops us from stepping into our own uniqueness and finding our individual voice?

Is fear holding you back?

For many people, a fear of change and the unknown can get in the way of finding their individuality. But what is fear? It could be described as False Evidence Appearing Real, meaning that we can be frightened of something that is not really a threat at all but just something we believe to be a threat. It is also said that we have nothing to fear but fear itself. Fear is a strong emotion that can be hard to fight and it can stop us venturing into the unknown. Or we may be tapping into the turmoil and confusion in the world, and some of the anxiety we feel may belong to the collective unconscious. If we are all interconnected, then of course we are going to feel the rippling effects of global events and the trauma and emotions that go with them, even if they are happening on the other side of the world. But we don't have to fear these emotions.

Fear can stop us from attempting something new. How many times have you been impressed by a fantastic idea and wished that you had come up with it? Although you might never have dreamed up that idea, there will have undoubtedly been times in your life when you have missed opportunities or ignored a good idea because you were afraid that you couldn't make it happen or that somebody else would do a better job than you. Or perhaps you just want to keep yourself small and invisible so that you fit in; after all, the biggest problem after fear of failure is the fear of success.

In truth, however, nobody can stop us from being ourselves and fulfilling our destiny, because the one person who gets in our way is ourselves. So, as I often quote in my coaching sessions: keep out of your own way.

Living life to the full

If life is a journey or a long and winding road, we have to enjoy the steps we take on the way, because by the time we reach one of our goals we will already be on to the next one. We must live life to the full and enjoy the exploration as it will add richness to our experience and what we have to say. I had been working with a group of people in their twenties and as we were walking out of the building at the end of the day I heard one of them say, 'All I want is for __ to happen and then I will be happy.' I had to tell him that in my experience he would be continually raising his expectations of himself and that it was never about achieving just one goal. Any successful person will tell you that. Life is about the journey, not the destination.

Recently, I was talking to an extremely successful business-man who had started with nothing. I was intrigued when he admitted that when things had been going well he secretly hoped that something dramatic would happen because he got bored when it all ran too smoothly! It made me realise that this is why millionaires are millionaires: they never entertain thoughts of failure, but continually strive to find the successful solution in whatever project they take on. They put failures down to learning opportunities and, undaunted, they pick themselves up and go off and try something new. Their motto for life is 'nothing ventured nothing gained'.

The question to ask yourself is: are you going to live your life vividly or opaquely? Will it be grey and straight or full of colour with its ups and downs? I don't believe that there is such a thing as a safe life. Even if you live your life small it doesn't mean something huge can't happen. Now is the time to live your dreams and look into all aspects of your life to bring fullness to your experiences.

BE YOURSELF AND DARE TO FIND OUT WHO YOU TRULY ARE

In these times of celebrity culture, we can easily fall into the trap of comparing ourselves to those in the limelight and feeling that we fall short of how we think they live and are as people. This means we feel less confident about ourselves, but finding our true self and recognising the aspects that make us individual is so empowering.

There is something very liberating about managing your own life, taking control of your inner critic and taking responsibility for yourself. Nobody else can, or should, do that for you. Life is a rollercoaster with its ups and downs, but we feel joy more acutely because we have also felt pain. We appreciate abundance more if we have also experienced the absence of something. If we can:

Dance as if no one is watching
Love like you'll never get hurt
Sing as if no one is listening
Live like it's Heaven on earth.

I believe we have found our personal voice.

......

Exercise: visualise your perfect life

1 Imagine that you could do anything you wanted.

2 Where would you live and how would you fill your days?

3 Give yourself some space to consider the possibility of fulfilling your dreams and expectations; in other words how would you find your voice and live the life you would like to live?

4 Now look at the steps you would need to take to achieve it.

......

Your inner critic, or ego, will constantly fight with your intuitive voice and tell you that if you dare to be different, dare to be you, then terrible things will happen to you. Yet the most successful people in diverse walks of life will tell you that they have been through challenging and difficult times on their journey and it was only because they never lost sight of their goal or vision that they succeeded. There is also a phrase that comes to mind: 'the gift of desperation'. Sometimes, it is only when our backs are up against the wall that we will push through to the next level.

Remember that it is a journey to success. You need the ability to keep going and never give up, despite the moments of despair and blackness and wondering how you are going to reap the rewards. But it's equally important to enjoy the ride rather than just focus on the destination. Improving our voice when we speak doesn't happen overnight, so it's important to focus on the fact that it's the progress that matters not the perfection – and our voice reflects our wisdom and life experience.

THE POWER OF SILENCE AND ITS LINK TO THE HERE AND NOW

According to the spiritual teacher and author Eckhart Tolle the reason we find it so hard to live in the present is because we are identified with our minds. Our minds are constantly chattering away and it leaves little room for stillness – the home of the soul. He says that when we come into contact with our soul through accessing stillness on a regular basis we gain true power and knowledge. We gain an inner peace and nothing that happens on the outside can shake us. Learning to be still in the moment can help us find our personal voice.

BE KIND TO YOURSELF

If you are busy beating yourself up on the inside, it will distract you from being in the moment and thinking about what you are saying. Being kind to yourself is about stopping the self-recriminations and self-criticism. Instead, learn to value yourself and treat yourself as you would a close friend. When you are kind to yourself you are accepting, and this helps you to grow more fully and self-confidently. People often confuse being thoughtful to oneself as an act of selfishness, but it is actually quite the reverse; if we dislike ourselves or disapprove of ourselves we will also find it difficult to receive kindness from others, because we feel undeserving.

Perfectionism is not an attribute, it simply means that you will never be good enough, whatever you do, and it will limit your ability to take pleasure in your life's successes. The more you can acknowledge how far you have progressed, combined with a more constructive approach to your achievements, the more likely you are to succeed.

Forget blame

Another liberating action is taking responsibility for yourself, not buying into the blame game. (The 'blame game' is when someone refuses to accept responsibility for something they are responsible for, so they deflect that responsibility by blaming someone or something else.) Know that each of us is master of our own destiny. Nobody can keep us small or divert us from our path unless we allow them to. No individual can 'make' us feel anything unless we buy into their game. Freeing ourselves from self-imposed traps is the key to discovering who we really are and what we are meant to be doing with our lives. In other words, finding our true voice.

Our personal voice is what makes the things we say unique and special. In the next chapter we will see how to communicate clearly with others so that our message will be understood and not misinterpreted.

3
Clear Communication

Whether we are in conversation with one other person or making a presentation to a group, there are several ways we can improve our approach so that we are communicating what we actually want the other person, or people, to hear. There are several aspects to clear communication, and they're not only to do with what we are saying.

For most of us communication is about how we verbalise our thoughts and feelings to other people, but research has shown that even with the power of words to support us we often communicate badly. Apparently, over 90 per cent of problems in the workplace are blamed on poor communication. Good communication is the secret of success, and in this chapter we will look at how to achieve this by improving our message and listening skills. As well as using your voice, the other essential elements to communication are non-verbal communication and body language – although we don't usually think about these. I'll be explaining how to project the right message in our non-verbal communication as well.

GETTING THE POINT ACROSS

Effective communication is when you convey your thoughts and ideas clearly. It sounds simple, but there are blocks and barriers that get in the way of successful speech. Communication is a two-way process: *you* want to say something; the *listener* has to understand it. A survey carried out by a business school with companies employing more than 50,000 staff showed that good communication skills were the number-one priority when it came to selecting managers. Of course, how we relate to our friends and family members is just as critical as communicating in the workplace. Being able to identify who you are talking to and what you want to say to them is a fundamental part of good, clear communication. However, as the following stories prove, sometimes things go wrong when you don't know who you are communicating with!

Communication calamities

There are numerous comedies based on misunderstandings and assumptions, but awkward situations can happen in real life too, such as this story from television presenter and author Fiona Armstrong:

> I was presenting on breakfast television and we were doing a live interview on child abduction. It was the two-minute break and, during that time, the floor manager brought into the studio my two interviewees: a mother whose child had been abducted (and safely returned, thank goodness) and a child psychologist who was to speak about the damage that could be done to youngsters and their families through this kind of experience.
>
> The floor manager then suddenly arrived with another person – an elderly lady – and popped her at the end of the

sofa, and put a microphone on her. I looked at my notes – definitely only two people to talk to! I tried to get the floor manager's eye.

'Who is it?' I whispered, not wanting to be rude to the recently arrived guest. He looked at his list and shrugged.

'I'll find out,' he said.

The next thing we knew, the director was speaking in my ear, 'Coming out of the break . . . five, four, three, two, one,' and that was it. The red light came on and the camera was live. So I read the introduction to the piece and got the mother to tell her story. Then I moved on to the child expert. By this time the producer was hissing in my ear, 'Enough of him – now bring in the lady on the end.' The problem was, who was she? Throughout the chat she'd been sitting there nodding and listening, but what role did she play in all this? I took a deep breath. 'And what do you make of this?' I asked. A very general question was the least dangerous route, I felt. She looked very serious.

'Well, as a mother and a grandmother, I think it's terrible that someone would take another person's child.'

I breathed a sigh of relief, 'Thank you very much and now we'll take another break.' As the floor manager took the microphones from each of the interviewees, I leaned across to her, 'I'm sorry I didn't introduce you – but who are you?' I asked.

'Well,' she said, 'I was a bit surprised to be here myself. My daughter works here and I came to look round. She left me sitting in this waiting room, and the next thing we knew a man came up and said: "You're on!" . . . but I have enjoyed myself.'

This is not an isolated incident. A taxi driver who was waiting in reception at the BBC was mistaken for an expert on the latest music technology downloads and whisked off to a news set. Bewildered, but believing it to be part of the job interview, he skilfully negotiated five minutes of live questions about a subject he knew nothing about.

Both stories prove that you have to be alert and in the present to deal with a difficult situation. Fiona was obviously experienced enough to think on her feet, and the man certainly proved that he could think quickly as well, but if we overlook the basics or make assumptions in our communications with people it can get us into trouble.

The dangerous territory of assumptions

Can you remember a time when you, or someone you know, have made an assumption that created amusing or awkward consequences? Although a lack of information might have a comic outcome, it can equally create a potentially difficult situation. Recently, I was media training in a national organisation and a woman told me about a classic scenario. She had been working in her job for just a couple of months, travelling around the country and visiting various sites. She was then told to attend a meeting at a particular location. It was hundreds of miles from her office, so she booked her tickets, cancelled her other appointments and was ready to head off on her long journey. Luckily, she asked one of her colleagues if they were travelling to the meeting by car or train and discovered that it was actually being held in the headquarters where she worked, but in a room named after the place she thought she was meant to be travelling to.

So to sum up this point, even if you know what you want to say and it seems quite clear and obvious to you what you are saying, it's important to consider the finer details of the message and check there are no ambiguities. Remember that what you intend to say or give out in your message could well be open to many and varied interpretations.

SENDING YOUR MESSAGE CLEARLY

Clear communication is critical if we want to be heard. It involves sending simple and unambiguous messages to the receiver, who will understand exactly what we mean and intend them to hear. It seems so simple, but communication breakdown is a fundamental problem in all walks of life.

Case Study: Merrick

My son Merrick was about 15 and going through the usual teenage problems, one of which was being fairly uninterested in the classroom and certainly about homework issues. I made it very clear on several occasions to the various teachers that I was willing to work with the school and keen that they should contact me if there were any problems. Well, they did contact me, but the message came far too late: I got a phone call to say that he had not done any history coursework for two years and that his exam was in a fortnight! This is a classic case of poor communication. Yes, I got the message, but two years too late! If they had contacted me immediately that situation would have been averted and my dear son would at least have stood some chance of gaining a history GCSE.

Ironically, people who work in the media are among the worst communicators internally, as I have discovered while working in newsrooms up and down the country. Having trained hundreds of people, I have found that the greatest problems are caused by poor communication and misunderstanding. Particular problems arise when we're talking to a group.

THE PROBLEMS WITH COMMUNICATING

Receiving the message
When we're speaking, what do listeners notice the most?

- 🔊 55 per cent of the message is transmitted by appearance and body language.

- 🔊 38 per cent of the message is transmitted through voice and delivery.

- 🔊 7 per cent of the message is what you actually say.

How much will your audience remember?

- 🔊 Your audience will forget 25 per cent of what you said after 24 hours.

- 🔊 After 48 hours they will have forgotten 50 per cent.

- 🔊 After four days they will have forgotten 80 per cent.

- 🔊 Only 20 per cent is likely to stay in their conscious awareness after that time.

Target your audience

So, how do you begin to be heard and understood more fully? First of all, it's important to identify your audience and target your message to them. Are they children, teenagers, students, the elderly, the general public? If it is a diverse group, think of key themes that will hook them all in. We have to find ways to ensure that our audience hears the key points we want to make, so think about your main messages and how you are going to deliver them. Remember not to overload your listeners with too much information. Here are a few tips:

1 Keep it simple.

2 Avoid information overload.

3 Say something memorable – give examples.

4 Sell the benefits.

5 Think about your delivery.

6 Don't lecture, but engage your audience.

7 Be receptive to their opinions and reactions.

Remember, your communication is successful only when the sender and the receiver understand the same message. Communication is about conveying your thoughts, ideas and feelings in a clear way. Unfortunately, many people struggle to communicate effectively. Individuals lose jobs and relationships because they are ineffective when it comes to spelling out how they are thinking and feeling. And of course this also applies to written communications, such as letters, emails or texts, not just the spoken word.

Plan ahead

There is always the risk that your audience will misunderstand what you are trying to say, or they may feel bombarded with too many messages. Planning what you are going to say before you start will help to get your message across effectively:

🔊 Why are you communicating this message?

🔊 Who is it directed to?

🔊 What is the message?

🔊 What are its key points?

◀)) How will you make the key points memorable?

◀)) Have you considered cultural issues, such as different behaviour or customs adopted by people in other countries or social, ethnic or religious groups that could create misunderstandings or offence?

◀)) Have you made any assumptions?

◀)) Which is the most appropriate channel to use? Should it be verbal, face to face, by phone/videophone, letter or email?

Use the above points as stepping stones to help you deliver a clear and focused message.

Adopt the right tone: being assertive

When we talk or write we need to be assertive rather than aggressive or passive. Assertiveness means being clear and direct, saying what you want to say in a reasonable tone of voice, which can come through just as clearly in the written word as well as verbally. I'll be covering assertiveness in more detail in Chapter 4.

THE BARRIERS TO CLEAR COMMUNICATION

It's not just what you write or say that counts. There are barriers that can trip you up if you don't give enough thought to how you want to say something and consider who you are saying it to. Some of the common ones are:

◀)) Lack of planning and focus.

◀)) Not having a clear enough intention.

◀)) Using the wrong medium; for example, sending an email when face-to-face communication would have been more appropriate.

◀)) Lack of knowledge.

◀)) Not considering the other person's point of view; in other words, lack of thought or sensitivity.

◀)) The way you deliver the message – either the language you use or the tone of your voice.

Our emotions

Generally speaking, if you are in a highly charged, emotional situation in your personal or professional life, it will be difficult to be clear and coherent, because you won't be centred. If your mind and emotions are in a turmoil, it will be difficult to convey a clear message.

'Owning' your statements

Choosing to use 'I' rather than 'you' will completely change the tone of your message. It's called 'owning your statements' and it avoids accusatory language that can result in the other person feeling defensive. If they feel defensive they are then more likely to react in a hostile way.

When you own your statements – by using 'I' rather than 'you' or 'we' – you are more likely to receive a coherent response from the person you are communicatir ⁻ith. Here are some examples:

'I am feeling upset/angry/hurt.'
'When . . . happened it made me feel . . .'

When you own your statements, it me?
on the receiving end can hear what you ɘ

belongs to you and you are not trying to inflict your opinion on someone else.

Sometimes, when we don't really want to say something, we might try to 'deflect' that on to the other person. So we ask them a lot of questions in the hope of getting the answer we want rather than saying it ourselves. In this way we are, in effect, hiding behind the questions, but that can just be a way of avoiding dealing with our own feelings. With an 'I' statement you can describe a situation and your reaction to it without including your judgement of the situation. This is because your judgement is your opinion or observation and is not necessarily one that will be shared by the person you are speaking to. Although describing how you feel about someone's actions or behaviour is your personal opinion, if you say it in the right way it can be valuable feedback for them.

Projecting our feelings onto others

Our messages often contain our own assumptions and feelings that we might then project onto others, but we cannot possibly know how others think or feel, so we must avoid this. Be wary of telling someone else how they are thinking or feeling, or that you know for sure what their intention is. By owning your statements, you can be honest and say what you feel; if you are feeling scared or angry, say so. Honest communication is clear communication. If there is a situation that makes you unhappy, but you continually suppress your negative feelings, they will come out one day, probably when you least expect them.

THE EXPLODING-DOORMAT SCENARIO

Many years ago I attended a workshop with my now ex-husband. In those days I was a people-pleaser (someone who never says no to anything), and although I felt I had been honest with him over the years, it was only during the seminar that my true feelings burst out. They shocked me more than anyone else in the room. The workshop facilitator was trying to get me to tell my husband how I really felt, and at one point he said, 'Joanna, you are white with rage!' It was a very uncomfortable feeling, but I knew he was right. I could feel all this previously dormant fury rising up through me and trying to find a way out. I also remember being glad I wasn't near the knife rack at the time!

Even though you may not express your emotions it doesn't mean that they don't exist. It's what I call the sub-text. Have you ever spent time with somebody who is being very 'nice' about something but actually underneath it you can feel their fury? Well, that pent-up repression is toxic, and one day – and you will never know which day that might be – it might just all come flooding out when you are least expecting it. People who try to be 'nice' all the time can actually be 'exploding doormats'; in other words, every time they say yes when they really mean no, their emotions will build up, and one day there will be some volcanic activity! (This subject is covered in more detail in Chapter 4.)

NON-CONFRONTATIONAL WAYS TO SAY WHAT YOU FEEL

Taking personal responsibility for your message is especially relevant when talking one-to-one. Own your feelings and thoughts, and don't project them onto the other person or try to make the feelings theirs; for example, if you say, 'I think you are stupid' or 'You are a bully', you will not get the response you seek. On the other hand, if you say, 'When you did that I felt . . .' or 'That situation has left me feeling . . .' you will open the way for a dialogue without risking accusing the other person and receiving a negative response.

I try to avoid phrases like, 'You make me feel', 'You made me think' or worse: 'You made me do . . .' or 'Because of you I didn't . . .' Remember that nobody can *make* us do anything. We are responsible for our own thoughts, feelings and reactions. Starting to take personal responsibility for our lives and our mental and emotional states is ultimately liberating and empowering. Just keep practising the 'I' word and you'll be surprised how confident that can make you feel.

Be confident

You need to be confident about your message and what you want to say without being reliant on the answer you get back. So, for example, if you have to deal with a situation that has been difficult for you and you want to tell the other person how you feel, it is important that you voice it in the right way, but you have to detach yourself from your expectations of how they might react. For years I suppressed my negative feelings and was always worried about saying something that might upset somebody else. But in the end I found I was losing my self-respect and would walk away from situations feeling angry with myself for not having found my voice and spoken up. My experience has shown me that speaking my truth is the important factor – and that matters a great deal more than the answer I might get back from the person I am saying it to.

In control but not controlling

Be aware of your own agenda, however, and try to make sure you are not controlling the other person. When you are honest about yourself and not trying to worry about what the other person is thinking or feeling that will create the foundation for clear and empowering communication.

WHAT CAN GET IN THE WAY OF YOUR MESSAGE?

Whoever we send our message to, whether it is one person or a group, the same obstacles can apply. It is important to be aware of any potential problems before you speak, so ask yourself the following:

- ◀)) How dependent are you on the answer you get? Are you relying on getting a particular answer?

- ◀)) Are you scared of the other person or their reaction, or are you trying to control them?

- ◀)) Are you making assumptions?

- ◀)) Is this something you have tried to say to them before, and if so, why did they not hear you?

If you answered yes to any of the above, you probably need to learn how to be more assertive. I will be explaining how to do this in Chapter 4. Always choose your words carefully and remember that they have the power to heal or hurt. Try to be positive, not negative.

Coping with a disability

Learning to communicate effectively may seem challenging for most of us, but if you have a disability that task can be even more difficult – and you also have to cope with other people's perceptions and prejudices. However, people succeed in getting their message across in the face of all kinds of communication barriers, as this inspirational story illustrates:

Case Study: Sarah

Sarah is 37 and has cerebral palsy:

'When I was little I shared a room with my older brother. I used to make some weird and wonderful noises, which he would copy. Then he reversed it so that I would copy the sounds that he made. His sounds became words, and I vividly remember him teaching me how to say "aeroplane". My brother broke the word into three syllables and I said each syllable after him. This is how I learnt to talk.

'During my early years I was in and out of hospital with severe asthma. Mum would ask the hospital not to do things to me unless she was there, but they still did. They would try giving me an injection or putting tubes up my nose, without telling me or explaining anything to me. My reaction was to scream and thrash about, because I hated what they were doing. I was scared and I wanted my mum. It was an extreme way of using my voice, nevertheless it was still using my voice to try and communicate something.'

Over the years Sarah has had to find different methods to communicate, and she says she sometimes finds it hard to talk to new people who are not used to her way of communicating. A great help has been a Lightwriter – a portable keyboard where you type in a message and it will speak it out – which is attached to her wheelchair. She can use it to type her answers to people. One of the most empowering situations for Sarah has been where she has interviewed her own carers through using this device.

What really struck me about Sarah when I met her was her independence and humour, and how she does not view herself as a person with problems. She lives independently, has plenty of social pursuits and does voluntary work for people she considers less fortunate than herself.

Not having a clear physical voice has not stopped Sarah from finding her own means of communication and living a full life. One of the biggest problems she faces is often the reactions of other people and their inability or discomfort at having to communicate with her. This proves that communication really is a two-way process.

If you have lost your sight

Blind or partially sighted people have their own particular problems with communication. We relate to others through all our senses, and our eyes play a vital part in that process. You can often tell more about what someone is really saying through their eye contact, or the lack of it, than through what they are saying. The story of Jill shows how her motivation to have a rewarding career paid off in spite of her loss of sight.

Case Study: Jill

Jill, who is now a radio presenter, went through the trauma of suddenly losing her sight at the age of 19, caused by a condition called diabetic retinopathy – an illness that left her completely blind in the space of just two weeks.

'The experience of sight loss left me feeling isolated and that I was a sighted person trapped inside this blind person's body.'

Jill found, to her dismay, that people generally didn't know how to handle her loss of sight.

'I remember when I first came out of hospital and I was standing next to my mum, and this person was saying, "Poor Jill, it must be so terrible." She was saying it as though I had died, not standing in front of her. That was the motivation for me to do something with my life.'

Jill started to rebuild her life, but was horrified by the reaction of potential employers to her sight loss. She was told that she would never do anything more than weave baskets or answer telephones for the rest of her life. In a bid to learn new skills she decided to get involved with hospital radio.

'To me it made sense that someone with no sight should be working with sound. It took me a further seven years of study, freelance work with newspapers and battling through job interviews, where it was obvious that I was deemed unemployable, to secure my job with Insight Radio, Europe's first radio station for blind and partially sighted people. It has been a lifeline for me, in that it has given me back my feeling of self-worth and my self-esteem. Through trying to educate others about living with blindness, I have found out so many things about myself. Even the tiniest little piece of information can make a huge difference to someone's life. If my show can help do that, then my journey with blindness has not been in vain.'

But Jill admits that it took six years of blindness for her to finally grieve about the loss of her sight.

'I was attacked in broad daylight by two men. Up until that point I thought I was invincible. I mean, I couldn't comprehend of anybody wanting to attack a blind person . . . I felt protected by my sight loss, but then there was this realisation that I couldn't see danger. This whole incident made me become more honest about how difficult it was to lose my sight. You miss what you once had. People who've been blind since birth say, "You can't miss what you haven't had."

'I try my best to be honest about my feelings. And being honest is about my finding my voice – and that I know is more helpful to others.'

Overcoming deafness

Deafness not only affects the person who has the hearing impediment but it also affects the people they need to communicate with. It can be a frustrating and isolating experience when you find it difficult to make yourself heard and understood because of hearing difficulties. Nicola was determined not to let herself be defined by her deafness and worked hard to overcome many obstacles and pursue an interesting career:

Case Study: Nicola

Nicola has been profoundly deaf since birth. Ironically, her lack of hearing seemed to me to be the least of her problems when she came to me for coaching. The main thing she and I worked with was getting her to admit that there was a problem at all, so that people would be able to communicate more clearly with her.

'One of my greatest fears was to be referred to as "the deaf one" – I never ever wanted my ears or my "disability" to be

the thing that defined me. I was born deaf. It's a hereditary condition, but because of my family situation it meant that I was the only hearing-impaired person I knew. There's no cure and my children are likely to have hearing impairments too, so really I should not only accept it but I should also own this aspect of me. After all, it is my deafness along with my forceful determination, my ambition and my desire to understand people that has led to me getting a dream career.'

Nicola says her determination to do well in spite of having hearing problems was often spurred on by others:

'My memories of teachers seems to be shaped by how they reacted to my hearing. Some will stick in my memory forever for their inappropriate comments: "So Nicola is hearing things now, is she?" when I began packing my pencil case as the school bell rang. Some were far too attentive and would irritate me with their constant checking. I would seethe inside when teachers insisted I move to the front so that I could hear, or stall the lesson by asking for my radio aids. Of course I needed to do this, but I was more than happy to do the work in my own time.

'College was pretty much the same; I would avoid making a statement about my needs and would struggle along or just ask my friends if there was anything I had missed. No one ever noticed that I hadn't heard a single word of the lesson, I got the grades and so I got away with not listening too! Half the time I was a daydreamer, because I could actually switch off from the world around me. I still am. Switching off my hearing aids and getting lost in a story has always been my favourite thing to do.'

Nicola says she believes her deafness and not wanting to stand out for the wrong reasons made her even more determined to do well. Perhaps what sums up her ability to communicate against all odds is that she has now become a broadcast journalist. After our sessions together she eventually conceded that perhaps her biggest problem is not her deafness but her reluctance to ask for help.

COMMUNICATING THE MESSAGE
IN BUSINESS

Research has shown that some of the biggest communication problems occur in the workplace. Having worked as an employee and as a trainer of managers, I have found that poor communication is often created by fear, and it tends to work from the top down; for example, if a manager has to deliver bad news to the team, he or she may have been told to withhold certain information from the staff and would then find it difficult to communicate with real integrity and honesty. This can leave the manager feeling guilty and glossing over issues.

Indeed, employers and their top staff consistently run away from delivering bad news. It's as if they feel that no news is better than bad news, but studies have shown time and again that staff would rather know what is going on in the organisation so that they can prepare themselves for a worst-case scenario.

In the workplace, there is no doubt that uncertainty can lead to poor productivity, low morale, absenteeism and serious levels of stress and illness, so it is in a company's best interests to be more forthcoming when they communicate with their staff.

The trauma of redundancy

I have often heard stories of people who have been told they have lost their job and that they must pack their bags and leave the building instantly. They feel that they have been treated as though they are criminals when actually the problem lies in the way the employers have communicated the situation to them. The whole issue of redundancy is difficult for the person whose responsibility it is to inform their staff, but it's essential that these situations are handled with sensitivity and care. Sometimes the message can be delivered in a very abrupt, emotionally insensitive way, or the manager might not consider the possible options they could offer the employee who might lose their job. Staff need to be told in a compassionate way, and there should be adequate support already in place for them. Otherwise staff will suffer from fear and worry, which adds to the problem of threatened redundancy. Many people who have been made redundant are left traumatised because of the way they were treated as they left the company, but this is mostly created by a breakdown in communications.

TOP TIPS FOR THE WORKPLACE

◀)) If you are a manager, communicate with your staff and give them feedback. Praise publicly but give any negative feedback in private. Constructive criticism is the key to improving your workforce's product and morale.

◀)) Be aware of how you deliver your message. It needs to be clear and thoughtful to be heard and understood.

◀)) Give examples to back up what you are saying, so that your team can understand exactly what you mean; generic statements or global criticisms will be lost or misconstrued.

◀)) If you need to criticise someone, it is better to sandwich the negative comments between two positive statements. This will make the criticism constructive rather than demoralising for the employee.

◆)) Be visible in the workplace. Don't just hide ᵇᵉʰⁱⁿᵈ your computer sending emails; they can often ᵇᵉ misunderstood, because it is difficult to write exactly the way you are thinking, and they lack the tone you would give your message if you were saying it. Ensure your communication is face to face when it is about an important issue.

◆)) Make sure you hear the other person's side of the story. If you don't give them a fair hearing you might not fully resolve the problem.

◆)) Always deal with problems as they come up. An employee can't change his or her behaviour or work pattern if no one has told them there was a problem in the first place.

◆)) Try to ensure there is a creative solution to any problem. Both parties should feel that they have had their say and been heard.

How to sell a product

Trying to get your message across clearly is essential if you are selling a product, but you can also use a similar technique in other situations. When giving a message to a potential customer, how can you ensure it will be heard? One of the classic ways to practise selling something is using what is known as the elevator pitch. It's a useful exercise in any situation where you need to plan and focus on what you want to say to someone. Here's how to use it:

Exercise: elevator pitch

1 Imagine you are in a lift and you bump into a venture capitalist. You want to arrange a meeting with them but you only have a couple of minutes to persuade them to see you at a later date. How do you do this? You only have a very short time before they get out at the next level.

2 You need to describe one key point about your business that will be remembered easily. This is called your unique selling point (USP): it's a very brief description about what is great about your business, how it will benefit the customer and what the financial gains are. Right, you've got 30 seconds to describe your USP.

3 Think about how you can get to the point quickly, not by talking fast but by being clear in the fewest possible words. The experts will tell you that if you haven't got your message across in that 30 seconds you will not get it across at all.

MESSAGES VIA EMAIL

Emailing has become a popular form of communication, both in the workplace and at home, because it is so useful and quick, saving you time that would be spent on the telephone. As its use increases, however, so do the potential problems that go with it. It's so easy to rush off an email that too often we've hit that send button having written something in haste and not thought about the message properly. What's more, it's easy to send it to the wrong person, or to press the 'reply all' button rather than replying to just one person. Although there are many potential minefields, however, the basic problem with an email is how easy it is for someone to misinterpret your message. That can be because of the tone of the email, the words you have used, or the context, or lack of context, in which you have said something. So, how do we overcome this?

1 Keep your message simple and don't write anything that could be misinterpreted.

2 Always read it through carefully before sending it.

3 If you receive an email that makes you mad, don't send a reply in haste or you may regret it. It's easy to misunderstand someone and then you could overreact and create problems that you then have to backtrack on.

4 Check that sending an email is the best means of communicating in this instance. Perhaps a letter or a phone call might be a better option, or even talking face to face.

LISTENING

Did you know that the words 'silent' and 'listen' have exactly the same letters in them? True listening is focusing on what the other person is saying to you, not interrupting or dreaming up your answer while they are talking to you. So to listen, you must be silent. Just as there is an art to sending a message, there is an art to receiving one.

THE ART OF LISTENING

1   Listen unconditionally: hear what the person is saying to you without your own personal agenda getting in the way; in other words, listen without being dependent on hearing a particular message but be open to what might be said to you without having already thought out your answers.

2   Look at the person and stay focused on what they are saying to you – don't let your attention wander.

3   Stay focused, pay attention and give non-verbal signs that you are listening, such as good eye contact and occasional nodding. Don't interrupt and don't judge.

4   Have you understood what has been said? Can you describe the key points?

5   Is it believable? Does it feel truthful? Is the message sincere and delivered with integrity?

6   Let the other person finish what they are saying and make sure you have been listening properly before replying. If you are unsure about what someone has said, don't be afraid to ask them to clarify it.

7   Think before you reply.

8   If appropriate, use reflective listening. This is when the listener clarifies what the other person has said to them by restating their words, although not by repeating them word for word. It is a technique people use to show they are listening and to check that they have heard correctly what the person intended them to hear. This can be particularly useful if you want to be supportive when someone is upset.

What gets in the way of listening?

Think about the blocks that stop you from hearing what someone is saying. Do you have your own agenda, or are you experiencing such high emotions that you don't want to hear what that person has to say to you? Perhaps you only hear what you want to hear. Be open and receptive to what the other person is saying.

Each person is unique, and various personality types will filter information from a message differently:

- ◀)) The logical person is more likely to react to words like 'thinking', 'explaining', 'deciding' and 'considering', 'process' and 'choice'.

- ◀)) The feeling, or kinaesthetic, person will be tuning into what is being said through their senses and feelings, and tune into words like 'touch', 'feel' and 'connect'.

- ◀)) The visual person will visualise pictures for the words they are hearing. Key words for this type include 'picture', 'imagine' and 'see'.

- ◀)) The auditory person will be more responsive to words like 'sound', 'hearing', 'attune' and 'listen'.

Start to become aware of how you listen; you'll find that it is harder to listen than to talk.

Case Study: Josh

Josh lived with his mother and three sisters. He was surrounded by their relentless chatting. Growing up, he felt he was not really able to get a word in edgeways. His mother noticed that as he reached his older teenage years he suddenly stopped listening to anyone and started to talk over people. She felt sure he had developed the habit because he felt he did not get the opportunity to say what he wanted to when he was younger.

Many years ago I attended a self-development seminar. The group spent some of the time sharing their experiences and working through various issues. As the weekend came to a close someone asked me what I did for a living. At that time I was a television newsreader. When I told them what I did, they exclaimed, 'Isn't that interesting; you never really felt heard in your life so you ended up broadcasting information to the nation!' I was quite stunned by their comment, but then I realised that it was partly true. It would be fair to say that I probably did not feel heard. This is because in the past I had been a people-pleaser and spent the whole time trying to say what I thought people wanted me to say rather than speaking my truth. Now that I work as a voice coach I have healed myself through helping others – and it has made the sessions more valid, as I can empathise with the participants and encourage them from the position of having been in a similar situation myself.

WHAT WE COMMUNICATE THROUGH BODY LANGUAGE

We often give away more about ourselves through our conscious or unconscious gestures than we do with what we say, and sometimes what we don't say will tell the other person more than any words can. To communicate effectively we need to read these non-verbal signs. Body language can often give others pieces of information about a person in addition to what they are actually saying. For our words to be credible, our body language has to match what we are saying, but our physical gestures can often reveal what is going on underneath – in our subconscious. The body is a signpost to our emotions.

Body language can be quite complex to interpret: we cry tears of joy and tears of sorrow, and sometimes even tears of anger; smiling and laughing are not always about expressing joy and happiness – they can be also be a way of conveying unkindness or sarcasm. When talking with someone, think about whether the words they are saying match their body language. Let's first look at the feelings we might have inside that tell us something about the person we are talking with.

Intuition: your inner alarm system

Your 'inner knowing' is vital when it comes to interpreting messages from another person. That 'knowing' feeling is your inner alarm system, and it will give you clear information from the 'energetic signals' you are picking up. (When you *hear* what the person has to say but *feel* they mean something different, these are 'energetic signals'. I call this the sub-text: something that's going on underneath and is not being spoken.) When I talk about your 'inner knowing' I'm talking about your intuitive self. This is the instinctive part of ourselves that will give us a nudge or a sign when we are talking to someone, or when we are in a certain situation, but the sign we receive might not correspond with the messages our other senses are picking up. So, for example, the person we are talking to may be smiling and saying positive things, but we may have a nagging doubt that all is not right. Our intuitive voice is our sixth sense, and it is as important as the other five, so we need to take notice of it. I know that whenever I haven't listened to my intuitive voice I have come to regret it.

Now let's take a look at how we can pick up non-verbal clues about someone.

Eyes

When communicating with others it is possible to be saying one thing but our eyes can be revealing something quite different. Our eyes are said to be the windows to our soul and they can reveal our inner truth, so if you are confident and genuine in what you are saying it will be reflected in your eyes. I often say to people I coach that they should tell the story with their eyes as well as their voice.

Many television presenters read from an autocue, but the art of good delivery is when they appear to be looking at you and not noticeably reading from the screen with their eyes glazed. Good presenters are connected to what they are saying, and this is the same for all of us when talking: if we are in the present moment, it will be reflected in our eyes. The person listening and watching will intuitively know that you mean what you are saying and that you are engaging with them.

Research has shown that our mood is reflected in the size of our pupils. Dilated pupils show excitement, whereas contracted pupils can be a sign that the person is shut down or not necessarily telling you the truth. When people appear cold and distant we see that in their eyes.

How to maintain eye contact without staring
People will become overly self-conscious and uncomfortable if you concentrate on their eyes when they are speaking. The way to maintain eye contact without staring into the eyes is to imagine that a person's face contains a triangle between the mouth and eyes. If you look in that area and shift your gaze between their eyes and lips, you will be making good eye contact without making them feel uncomfortable. Focus more on what you are saying to them, and you will not hear your own inner critic (page 8), which may get in the way of your message.

If you are facing a large audience, you might worry about where to look. Even if it feels unnatural to begin with, try to look in the direction of everyone in the room. Even if it is only a fleeting acknowledgement, it will make people feel included.

Open body language

Aiming for what is known as open body language is preferable to closed body language, which, as the word suggests, means being closed in on yourself. Closed body language is when you use your arms or legs as a kind of barrier. If someone is sitting hunched up and gazing at their feet, it is not exactly a welcoming gesture for open communication. Open physical gestures and good eye contact, however, will help you deliver a clear and confident message.

If you feel at ease, the other person will feel at ease too. So, be responsive and reflective; demonstrate that you are listening to them. A smile or a nod can be encouraging, especially if the person is giving a talk or demonstration. Avoid using any barriers, such as folded arms or clenched hands, as these will be off-putting and not make anybody feel at ease.

Positive signs include:

- ◀)) Open body language and relaxed gestures.

- ◀)) Good eye contact and thoughtful expressions.

- ◀)) Leaning towards the person rather than away from them.

- ◀)) Relaxed, but attentive, body language.

Negative signs include:

- ◀)) Poor eye contact; holding your hand over your mouth.

- ◀)) Clenched fists.

- 🔊 Leaning away from the speaker.

- 🔊 Doing distracting things, such as tapping a foot, sucking a pencil or looking bored.

READING BODY LANGUAGE

Closed body language is a barrier or defensive gesture that the other person is displaying. Certain facial expressions are also barriers:

- 🔊 If someone crosses their arms, it can be a sign that they feel threatened or worried and are trying to protect themselves, especially if they fold both arms across their chest.

- 🔊 When someone crosses their legs, it can be seen by others as a negative action, even though it is something that many of us do.

- 🔊 Clenched hands are a sign of frustration and sometimes anger.

- 🔊 When someone covers their mouth, it's a sign of guarded behaviour.

- 🔊 If they rub their eyes or ears, it is said to be an indication that the person does not want to 'hear' what is being said.

- 🔊 Pursed lips, tension around the eyes or a false smile are all tight facial gestures which act as barriers.

How to work with the barriers of body language

There are some schools of thought that suggest you should mirror the other person's body language to make them feel more comfortable in your presence, but I disagree. Having to work out what body language to mirror would just confuse me and distract me from listening. I vote for being in the present moment and genuinely responding to what the other person is saying rather than acting it out like a bad script in a play.

CLARITY

Here is a word that encapsulates confident body language and listening skills.

C   is for being centred.
L   is for looking at the other person and making good eye contact.
A   is for assertive non-verbal communication.
R   is for responding to what the other person is saying.
I   is for being intuitive and picking up vibes from others.
T   is for thinking clearly and being in the moment.
Y   is for being yourself which ensures natural and confident body language.

In the next chapter I explain how you can improve your communication by being assertive. Finding your unique voice comes from self-confidence, and being assertive means that you will be able to express more clearly and firmly what you mean without appearing to be aggressive.

4
Assertiveness Skills

I n the last chapter I explained how communicating clearly will ensure that the message you send is the one that is heard by the person listening. In this chapter I will explain how being assertive makes us stronger and able to express our own personal voice, so that we are communicating even more effectively. Assertiveness is a form of communication that recognises respect and integrity. It is a way of expressing thoughts, feelings and beliefs clearly so that they do not undermine or violate someone else's. It is about having the confidence to speak clearly without trying to put the other person down.

There are three other behaviours that many people use to communicate: aggressive, passive and indirect. I'll be discussing how to avoid these and how to deal with them in other people.

It's surprising that so many people confuse assertiveness with aggressive behaviour. I have often heard people say, 'I know I need to be more aggressive', when what they actually mean is that they need to stop being passive and to say what they truly feel or mean. This is not being aggressive; it is asserting your truth in a clear and confident way.

WHY IT'S IMPORTANT TO BE ASSERTIVE

Although it's great to be popular and willing to help others, we also need to have boundaries and know when it's the right time to say no. This is fundamentally about being able to take personal responsibility and not buying into the blame game. We should start by looking at ourselves and not others.

Being assertive is about being honest and having clear, direct communication. It is not about blaming others or being controlling or bossy. Neither is it about demeaning others or dumping the responsibility onto someone else. Being assertive is about respecting yourself and other people.

As explained in Chapter 3, one of the most powerful ways of speaking our truth and commanding respect from others is 'owning' what we say. How many times have you heard people talk about 'you' or 'we' when they're expressing something that *they* feel? This is expressing their own opinion rather than the other person's, and it is almost guaranteed that speaking this way will alienate others and build up hostilities.

Listening and compromising, while owning what you say

Being assertive means being willing to listen to the other person and being prepared to compromise. Just because you feel strongly about something doesn't necessarily mean you're right. Owning your statements helps you to be aware of your feelings and to respond in a clearer and more authentic way. You cannot be judged or blamed for having feelings. You have the right to your feelings and the right to express your beliefs and opinions. You also have the right to ask for what you need and the right to change your mind.

BEING HEARD

There are countless situations where people want to confront an injustice and have their say, but they don't know how to deal with it. How can you speak without causing the situation to escalate? The most important thing to remember is not to become combative. If you accuse the other person of something (even if you believe it's true) they will go on the defensive or shut down and will simply not hear what you are saying. The way forward is to remember to use the word 'I' and to own your feelings without accusing the other person. Here's how:

'When you did . . . I felt . . .'
'I felt . . . when this happened'
'That experience left me feeling . . .'

Coping with bullying

Unfortunately, I have worked with countless people who felt bullied in the workplace. It is a common problem and one that can cause a great deal of distress if it isn't dealt with, but most people do not know where to start, or they approach it in a way that will just make matters worse.

Case Study: Steve

Steve felt constantly picked on and undermined by his boss, and at times he had been accused of things he felt he had not done. He was ready to confront his boss and tell him that he was a bully. I pointed out that if he accused his boss in this way he would simply go on the defensive, shut down and probably become aggressive. I suggested that instead Steve should go to see his boss having researched his case and give clear examples without the language of blame. He took my advice and used an example followed by his own feelings and reaction to the situation to make his point. It worked, because it was easier for the person on the receiving end to hear a fact (that is, an example) followed by the feeling, which he could not argue with, so it left him clear to hear what was really being said. So, Steve was able to be assertive and achieve a good result from someone who often behaved in an unpleasant way.

The power of 'I'

Using the 'I' message rather than the 'you' message deflates a potentially difficult situation. We can use it to illustrate the feelings we have and the incident that sparked them in a clear and dispassionate way. Assertiveness means stating the facts and owning your feelings without judgement. Here's another example:

Instead of saying: 'You make me upset when you don't help.' It would be better to say: 'I feel upset when you don't help with [*and give an example*].'

It is important to separate the individual from their actions. So if you are dealing with a difficult teenager (and I have had plenty of experience in that department!) hurling accusations at them won't work, because teenagers simply don't hear. If you throw judgements such as 'You are stupid/lazy/rude', and so on, they are not going to listen or do anything other than shout back or ignore you. But if you give an example of a time when they were rude or lazy and tell them how that made you feel, they are much more likely to respond and do something about it.

Being specific

Often people are in denial about their behaviour patterns, so you need to be specific in order for them to understand what you are saying. Generalising or hurling accusations will come over as unfair criticism without any evidence.

Beware of assuming that other people know how you are feeling. In my experience most people are too self-obsessed to be worrying that much about you. Unless you tell them, how can they know how you feel or do anything to change what they are doing that upsets you? You must learn to value yourself enough to give honest feedback. When you speak, ensure that you say it in a way that is going to be heard, and then you are more likely to get a positive reaction.

When you need to repeat yourself

Another trap that individuals fall into is the one of constant repetition. Some people might call it nagging or controlling. If you feel you are not being heard, or you are unhappy about somebody's behaviour, you may have to talk to them about it on more than one occasion, but if you do it in an assertive way the message will eventually get through. Most people are so worried about their own business that they are not necessarily going to remember something you have told them, particularly if it is about a bad habit they have got into. Try the art of gentle persuasion – it works.

GETTING THE BENEFIT OF FEEDBACK

One of the greatest problems I have encountered as a communications coach in the workplace is the lack of feedback people get from their managers, or the way in which any feedback is delivered. If you believe that not giving feedback is a way to avoid an issue, you're wrong. Being a reformed people-pleaser, I know how tempting it is to say only positive things to people and to avoid what really needs to be said. But I have coached so many people over the years who bemoan the fact that nobody gives them feedback.

I had been training staff at one particular news organisation for many years and I remember on one occasion going to the see their boss and telling him that his staff were delighted with his regular and positive praise but they were desperate to hear the areas in which they could improve. He looked very bemused, but then later admitted he found giving critical feedback difficult. I suggested he looked at the whole issue in a different light; after all, how could any of his staff raise their game and improve if nobody told them where they were going wrong? He then realised that feedback was essential for an efficiently run operation and for the morale of his staff.

When you deliver difficult feedback in a positive way, you will be heard and the message will be received. Constructive feedback delivered in an assertive way will make the listener feel valued and able, with knowledge, to move forward and improve. One assertive way to give feedback is to start by commenting on something good the person has done and then point out the issue that you are not happy with, but end your feedback on another positive note.

ACCEPTING COMPLIMENTS LIKE GIFTS

Until someone pointed out to me that I should accept compliments, I didn't realise how rude, arrogant and opinionated I had been by not accepting them. Think about how you receive flattery or praise. When you are told you look good or smart, and so on, do you accept the compliment graciously or do you protest too much?

Imagine someone gives you a beautiful present. You would not turn round and say you didn't want it – that would seem extremely rude and dismissive. You should see compliments in the same way. Another person has bothered to tell you something that should make you feel good about yourself, but you have thrown it back in their face. If you do that too often they will soon give up on the praise.

Imagine how it feels for them. It can be hurtful to be dismissed in this way, and, after all, your self-deprecation is your problem, not theirs. What is more, by pushing the compliment away you are basically saying that you know better than they do. It is an arrogant form of behaviour, and it is telling the other person that you value your opinion above their own. For years I rejected compliments and reacted to praise as though it were a damning insult, but when I looked carefully I realised that the compliment made me feel better and the person giving the compliment felt better as well.

As a coach I can see and feel the exasperation when someone will insist they are terrible when you are trying to give them positive feedback. It is draining, exhausting and pointless for both parties. Rejecting praise and positive feedback can be one of the most serious forms of sabotage to clear and effective communication. So, remember to accept with grace. It will make everyone feel better.

Exercise: how do you receive compliments?

1 Think about how you have accepted compliments in the past. Do you like to receive them or are they rather embarrassing?

2 Do you deflect the praise and turn it into a negative? For example, if someone says you look attractive today, do you then use it to put yourself down by saying something

like, 'Oh, I'm having a bad hair day'? Or if someone says they like the clothes you are wearing, do you say something like, 'I just got them in a bargain sale'?

3 Do you feel you have a negative image of yourself, which makes it difficult to accept a compliment by just saying, 'Thanks'?

4 Remember that if you keep handing a compliment straight back, people will stop giving them to you.

5 Make a conscious effort to think about your response in the future when people give you compliments. They are given to make you feel happier, so enjoy the feeling.

AGGRESSIVE BEHAVIOUR

We have probably all been on the receiving end of someone insulting us or blaming us for something we haven't done. Often it is the way in which it is said that can be the most damaging. Aggressive behaviour can make you feel blamed, put down or even threatened. When someone gets into your personal space, or you feel invaded verbally or physically, that is aggressive behaviour.

Unfortunately, many people resort to aggressive behaviour when they feel insecure and don't know how to communicate clearly. This kind of behaviour is when someone expresses their opinion as a fact, which makes you in the 'wrong'. Aggressive behaviour is when someone is harsh or sarcastic, or when they invade your space and use threatening body language, and there is usually no space for you to reply.

Remain calm

If we are clear and confident about what we have got to say, there is no need to be pushy or demanding. Also, if we have inner confidence, we will be less worried or threatened by the other person. If it does happen, remember to give yourself space to think clearly and take a breath before you speak, and always respond in a calm and assertive way. When people behave in an aggressive way they are dogmatic and bullish and believe they are right and you are wrong, but you will not necessarily get the right of reply if you are up against that kind of behaviour. Aggressive behaviour is about threatening, dominating and bullying others, and often that kind of person will work along the lines of 'do as I say but not as I do'. Their language will maim and shame the person on the receiving end of it. So, it is important to learn how to deal with people who display this kind of behaviour pattern. You need to possess the inner assertiveness to know that it is not your problem but theirs. Here's are some aggressive phrases:

'You're stupid!'
'You shouldn't have done that.'
'Don't answer me back!'
'I'm the boss; do as I say!'

Basically, someone who is aggressive will attempt to get the other person to behave passively and not to stand up for themselves. This, of course, is bullying and intimidation, and although the aggressor might feel that they have won, in actual fact the only reason nobody stands up to them is through fear rather than respect.

One way that can help you deal with an aggressive person is to remind yourself that he or she is the one who feels insecure and frightened at some level. They are trying to control others as a way of keeping their own anxieties in check, and what they are doing is projecting their problems and worries onto you. It's often very hard for people to admit a problem or to say they can't cope and to invite help.

PASSIVE-AGGRESSIVE BEHAVIOUR

When someone behaves in a passive-aggressive way this is no better than aggressive behaviour. It is simply a way of expressing negative feelings in an indirect or silent way. An example of this would be a boss who promises promotion but never delivers. He or she might think that by assuring an individual that they are going to get a pay rise or a better position the person will perform better in the workplace, when in actual fact they have no intention of following this through.

Passive-aggressive behaviour is when actions speak louder than words: someone might use flattery or praise but it feels completely insincere to the listener. When a person masks their anger because they are unable to express it properly, it can be dressed up by insincerity or a lack of action. But it is still aggressive, although more subtle – and the consequences can be devastating.

Passive-aggressive behaviour can be even more toxic than openly aggressive behaviour, because the person might appear to embrace your idea or request so that you are fooled into believing something is actually going to happen. From my experience, passive-aggressive behaviour can be an extreme form of people-pleasing: saying what you believe that person wants to hear without thinking through the consequences of that action.

PASSIVE BEHAVIOUR

Are you the person who usually ends up saying yes and often shouldering other people's responsibilities? Well, although it might make you popular, you probably won't be respected for it – and, more importantly, you won't feel good about yourself. How many times have you said yes when you really wanted to say no? How many times have you felt that you have not been heard? This is passive behaviour: it makes us feel undervalued and turns us into victims. You will always know the kind of people who can't stand up for themselves; they are the ones that are exploited and put upon by others.

COLLECTING STAMPS

One of my favourite analogies to describe the path of passive behaviour is the book of stamps. If you are someone who has a tendency to say yes and to want to please others, it is very likely you are building up a large book of stamps. Every time you say yes, when you really want to say no, that is an unspoken stamp of resentment going into your book. It could be anything from agreeing to do the extra shift that nobody has volunteered for at work to managing the cake stall at the school fair when you really wanted to do something else.

The more you avoid dealing with your resentments, or you say yes when you really mean no, the more the toxic resentments that haven't been dealt with are building up. You might even be unaware of the build-up because you have become so used to being uncomfortable. You have learned to hide away and avoid your real feelings rather than saying what you want to say, so the stamps of resentment are adding up in that book. But inevitably, one day, probably when you least expect it, the last stamp will go into your book and you'll reach the end of your tether and lose your temper. Everybody else is, of course, stunned by your unreasonable behaviour over such a small thing. After all, you have always said yes before, and you are the one that everyone else relies on. What's wrong? How dare you?

Of course, you have not just lost your temper over this one incident. It is an accumulation of toxic resentments that have built up over the past weeks, months or even years. The underlying truth is that we need to be able to be honest and say what we feel *at the time*. But having said that, there are appropriate ways to communicate, as I have been describing here.

Case Study: Elaine

I worked with Elaine, who was very conscientious and liked by everyone who knew her, but by her own admission she was a terrible people-pleaser. Although we used to have many informal coaching sessions, and I would try to persuade her not to allow people to take advantage of her so much, it wasn't until Elaine reached her own 'rock bottom' that things changed – or perhaps I should say before she changed her passive-behaviour patterns.

'A few years ago I read in my Chinese horoscope that success would come to me later in life. As the clock ticks towards my fiftieth birthday I look back on a shy, reserved girl whose knees

would tremble at the first sight of authority: the teacher, the boss, the GP, and even the librarian.

'It never occurred to me that anyone would listen or be interested in anything I had to say. I went quietly and steadily about my education and career – always smiling, willing, efficient and conscientious, but always in the back seat and never the driver.

'Popularity is never a problem for a people-pleaser, be it agreeing to that extra task when you're already creaking under the pressure, or accepting the blame for something you're not responsible for, because it's easier than voicing your own opinion or entering into a confrontation.

'I've been on countless gatherings, sipping warm white wine and nodding enthusiastically with the general consensus of opinion, when deep down I've wanted to cry out with my own opinion but never had the courage.

'So, what hope is there for life's doormat? An awful lot, is the answer. But no one is going to hand anything to you on a plate. You have to dig your heels in, grit your teeth and search your soul to find your inner confidence and self-assurance. You'll find that you will receive more respect from your family, friends, colleagues and peers than you ever imagined.

'As predicted in the Chinese horoscope, my turning point has been a long time coming, but after being shaken rigid by a misunderstanding in the workplace, I pulled myself up, dusted myself down and fought on inch by inch with hard work, self-respect and, most of all, humility. I drew my own boundaries, but that did not mean I had to change the person I am.

'As ever, I endeavour to please and I love to be liked, but I am not a "dumping ground". You can still be "you" and achieve the success you strive, both personally and in your career. People do listen to what I have to say and they want to hear my opinions, and, furthermore, I always stride confidently towards the librarian with my late returns!'

Don't be the exploding doormat

Do you remember the exploding-doormat scenario in Chapter 3? It's another example that illustrates what happens when you fail to deal with negative problems as they arise. In the past that has been a familiar feeling for me: walking away from a situation in which I wished I had been honest and spoken my truth. Feeling angry but not being able to acknowledge or express it can lead to simmering feelings of resentment, anger, self-pity and victimisation, which fester away but invariably leak out eventually.

How often have we walked away from a situation thinking about what we wished we had said? It usually comes to us in glorious and vivid technicolour! But it's all a drama in our heads, because the moment when we could have spoken up for ourselves has been lost. That's passive behaviour: not defending ourselves. It's about low self-esteem and powerlessness. If you over-apologise or are over-placatory, that's being passive.

Have you ever been around someone who appears to be very sweet and willing but you actually pick up some sense of their resentment? Unexpressed feelings and an inability to set boundaries can create very negative feelings which, if not dealt with, become toxic and block us from communicating clearly with others.

I have been guilty of regularly over-apologising and have spent many years trying to stop saying sorry or putting myself down out of sheer bad habit. According to my family and friends, I slip into this mode nowadays only when I'm feeling insecure or worried about something. Often the way we speak and the words we use can be a barometer of how we're feeling on the inside. These days I try to communicate with others by meaning what I say and saying it clearly and fairly.

INDIRECT BEHAVIOUR

When you avoid communicating clearly, so that the person you are talking to doesn't really know what you are getting at, this is called indirect behaviour. It's a form of passive behaviour, and when we use it we often resort to manipulation to avoid having to say something honestly. When someone is being indirect they are usually saying everything except what they really want to say. However, if you don't take the risk of communicating clearly, you will hold on to unhealthy feelings, just as with passive behaviour, and eventually you will end up lashing out at the person or going into some meltdown behaviour pattern.

People can avoid saying what they really want to say in lots of ways: they might talk in circles, never really getting to the point, or use humour to try to make their message more palatable. Some people will spread rumours or tell other people what they really want to say to a person rather than saying it out loud. One woman I know often says 'only joking' at the end of a statement. I have challenged her by saying that I don't think she is joking and that she really does mean what she is saying but is uncomfortable about voicing it. So when you're speaking your truth it's important to say what you need to say in a clear way that will be heard and understood by the other person.

TAKING PERSONAL RESPONSIBILITY

The more personal power we have, the more clear and direct our message will be to the outside world. Our message will also be more assertive when we feel comfortable and confident with ourselves. In the last chapter I talked about body language. Your body shows how you are feeling and becomes a part of your message. If you see someone slumping, with their eyes to the ground, you know they're not feeling good. When they are happy, it shows in their facial expressions and body language. I also explained about eye contact; when you can 'look someone straight in the eye' this shows you are confident and feel able to reveal yourself. As you gain confidence your demeanour will be positive and your message will be clear.

Personal responsibility is about feeling able to hold your hand up and admit when something has not gone the way you planned it, without feeling the need to cast the responsibility on to someone else. In all the team-building and communication-skills workshops I have run, the real breakthroughs are when an individual takes personal responsibility for, or simply recognises, the part they've played in their own success or downfall. Personal power is the courage to look at yourself in the mirror and know you have treated others in a way you would like to be treated yourself, and that you are honest with yourself.

YOUR INNER VOICE

A key way to finding your assertive and clear voice is to deal with your inner voice. By that I mean the voice of your ego as opposed to your intuitive voice. The voice of the ego can keep us too big or too small. The voice of intuition, however, offers us true guidance, but we can only access it if we are still enough to hear it. Developing one's sense of self comes from the inside, and the more conscious and aware we become of ourselves and our personal journey the more in touch we will be with our inner voice. Often that inner voice is a critic, which doesn't offer constructive feedback but feeds us with endless pointless chatter that makes us doubt ourselves and gets in the way of delivering our assertive message.

RECOGNISING YOUR INNER CRITIC IS AT WORK

Have you ever stopped to think about what you're saying to yourself?

- Is it positive or negative?

- Is it empowering or disempowering?

- Does it make you feel good about yourself or chip away at your self-confidence?

- Do you get in your own way?

Why you have to take control

It's no good trying to convey a positive message if you still have negative messages on the inside. How we see ourselves and what we say to ourselves can become self-fulfilling prophecies, so we need to crush that inner critic if we are to enjoy confidence and express ourselves effectively. There are different ways in which we can boost our self-esteem so that we can find our personal voice and be more assertive:

1 Learn to walk your talk; in other words, do as you say and lead by example.

2 Believe in yourself.

3 Fake it to make it.

Walk your talk
It makes no sense to make statements about the way people should live and behave if you then don't follow your own

advice. But it's easy to fall into that trap; for example, if you're shocked by people who cause accidents because they drink and drive, but you still drive when you've had a drink, that is an example of not walking your talk. And many parents are guilty of correcting their children of certain behaviours but then doing similar things themselves. Ultimately, though, you don't need to convince people about anything; you just live by example – it's the most powerful way of finding your voice.

Believe in yourself

However hard it is to be confident and clear, it's a process that can be learned, and if we have spent most of our lives doubting ourselves, we need to start believing in ourselves and talking clearly. Even if we don't match the positive message we are hearing on the inside to start with, eventually we will.

Fake it to make it

Once we start believing in ourselves we can 'fake it to make it'; in other words, when you turn down the volume on the negative talk and turn up the volume on the positive you will start to feel good about yourself rather than full of doubt. And once you start to feel good about yourself you'll move forward in life and benefit in many ways. Only you can choose what you listen to – it's just like tuning into a radio station of your choice – so make it the positives. Remember, the more you think positively the more comfortable you will become, and eventually assertive behaviour will be natural and instinctive. It might take a little while, but remember that you are on a journey and it is impossible to achieve goals instantly – that is part of the joy of being human.

WHAT HAPPENS WHEN YOU AVOID CONFRONTATION

For many years I tried to avoid any kind of confrontation. I tried desperately at home and in the workplace to create a harmonious atmosphere at any price. In the process not only did I collect hundreds of books full of resentment stamps but I now recognise that what I was doing by not being honest with myself or others was in some way unethical. If we don't value ourselves we are unlikely to value others, so if we are not being honest with ourselves, others will also be affected. When you avoid dealing with a situation or telling a friend, relative or colleague how you feel, you are in effect stockpiling trouble – and that isn't helpful to the other person.

Case Study: Laura

In one company I worked with, a young employee, Laura, asked me to go to the HR department with her because she wanted to lodge a complaint about someone else at work. I told her that I wouldn't do that but that I would help her to deal with the situation. In essence, her boss had said something that had hurt her, but it seemed to me that it had been said in the heat of the moment, while she was under a lot of stress. I pointed out to Laura that it was important to tell her boss what it felt like to be on the receiving end of those barbed comments.

We worked out how Laura could tell her boss directly how she felt. She used sentences like, 'When you said/did . . . I felt . . .', rather than using the language of blame, but gave clear examples of how her boss's behaviour had affected her. Laura took responsibility for her feelings and reactions, and in doing so the manager understood the impact of her own behaviour. Hopefully the experience helped her as a new manager to learn how to be a better team leader.

If we avoid telling someone that something is wrong because we want to avoid confrontational situations, how can that person ever change or learn from experience? We could be nursing a grievance for months and the other person would be oblivious. So, part of our personal responsibility is to speak out in these kinds of situations – remembering, of course, that the way we say it will make all the difference. Using non-confrontational terms will diffuse the situation so that both parties can move on.

Carrying our rucksack of problems around with us

Our personal life is intertwined with our work life, and one affects the other. We might feel that we can leave our problems at home when we go to work, but in reality we don't. Even if you don't verbalise something that is troubling you, your actions and body language will probably give the game away, and it could come out in a destructive way rather that a constructive one. The problem is that we carry our problems around with us in a kind of heavy, but invisible, rucksack. If we avoid confrontations at home, for example, we will undoubtedly be carrying them into the workplace. If something gets awkward there we might then overreact to it.

Stand firm – it could affect your future

Certain situations, such as wedding preparations, can be particularly stressful and might cause confrontational situations to arise. The following story shows that it is not necessarily your partner that you might have a confrontation with at this time.

Case Study: Jane

Jane had to break a lifelong pattern of submissive behaviour with her parents as they tried to take over her wedding plans.

'My husband-to-be and I had decided that we wanted a low-key wedding in a hot climate. The important thing to us was that we were making the commitment to each other, and if we could combine that with a fantastic once-in-a-lifetime holiday, then all the better. My parents had other ideas, and they had very clear views about the type of wedding we should have. Specifically, it should be a white wedding in a church and it would include distant family that my parents hadn't seen in over ten years and whom my boyfriend had never even heard of, let alone met. Their aim was to help mend a family feud! They said that they would be willing to contribute financially to the cost of the wedding if their wishes were followed.

'My fiancé and I were determined not to be railroaded into a wedding ceremony that met my parents' dreams and aspirations but not our own. And the last thing we wanted was a wedding day that we both looked back on with regret.

'I knew that I had to find my voice. And I did. We had a wedding abroad and my parents did not come. Yes, there was fallout and stress, but my husband and I both felt we had done the right thing, and we have not regretted it.'

Jane spoke up for herself and faced a difficult situation rather than simply giving in, and is now happy to have had the wedding she and her husband wanted rather than give in to her parents' wishes and regret it in the future. The story illustrates how important it is to face situations and to speak up for yourself. The feeling of strength and liberation you get when you do has continued benefits. In Jane's case being assertive and clear has given her an insurance policy for the future: her parents now know that she and her husband will make their own decisions in life. When you please someone else against your own needs, it simply keeps them trapped in their own negative and destructive behaviour patterns. If she had given in, her marriage might have ended before it began.

The courage to leave destructive situations

How we find our voice can be critical and in some cases your life might depend on it. Working as a crime reporter I was amazed at the courage people have shown when they have found their voice to confront very challenging situations by leaving them. In every situation, however harrowing, the victim had to find their voice to leave the violent home and nobody else could make them do that. Even in a situation like that it is the inner confidence that will lead you to find your assertive voice and speak up.

Case Study: Helen

Helen was married with two children, but she had a difficult domestic situation with her husband, who had started to be violent, and this made her very unhappy. She forgave him on each occasion because she always hoped he would revert to the way he was when she met and fell in love with him with at university. Her story illustrates how complex and difficult it can be to find our voice:

'The first time he punched a hole in our wall, I should have left. I was too scared to admit failure and too scared to be alone. The downward spiral really started.

'Then we had our first child. My pregnancy wasn't planned but we were happy. On the outside our marriage looked perfect, *but that was because I was very good at showing a public face. People never knew our issues. The day we brought home our firstborn I will never forget. He carried her to our bedroom and put her onto my lap and then gave me a gun magazine and asked if we could order his new gun.*

'I stayed with him. Maybe it was because it was now even harder to leave with the baby. The next year he was given an opportunity to move into a company house for free so that we could rent out our own house. It sounds perfect on paper, but the emotional consequences of that move led us ultimately to split up. When we moved he mentally "divorced" me and "married" his job. I was the trophy wife with one child and another on the way. His job took priority over everything – even over our family. He still had a fiery temper and we were also getting into debt.

'I don't know why I couldn't speak up to him about his temper, and the lack of family time he gave us. The fear of losing everything was too much. Our marriage sank to an all-time low. There was daily bickering and fighting, yet I still didn't stand up to him.

'My friend told me to stick it out for the next 18 years for the sake of the kids, and then get divorced. I was shocked at how many people thought that way. If I did that my children wouldn't be guaranteed a loving and safe environment for the next 18 years. The final straw was when he told my small children that I hated them. I knew then that I had to go, and I have not regretted making that decision.'

For a long time Helen stayed in that unhappy situation in the hope that it might get better, but in doing so she was avoiding confrontation. Once she fully realised that her husband's behaviour was unacceptable, she was able to confront the situation and find the strength to leave. Finding your voice in situations like this begins with admitting there is a problem;

nt of the problem then goes away and everything omes more manageable.

story illustrates the point that finding your voice and speaking up for yourself can be challenging and difficult. Sometimes the rewards will come a long time later, but you have to listen to the intuitive guidance that we all have and do what is right for you, because nobody else can, or should, do that for you.

The elephant in the room

You may have heard the phrase 'the elephant in the room'. This usually refers to a massive problem that nobody wants to acknowledge is there. Even though we all know the problem is there, we feel that if we don't talk about it we can pretend it doesn't exist, and we try to deal with little problems around it but ignore the main one. If this is happening in your life, don't allow the elephant to get bigger and take up more space, as eventually the room will not be able to contain it. As I have discussed throughout this chapter, we need to talk about the elephant in a way that will be constructive. Being assertive, not aggressive, is the way to speak out about difficulties so that they can be dealt with.

MOVING FORWARD

I want to conclude this chapter by reminding you of the best possible way to communicate assertively: it is essentially about finding a good resolution without blaming or offending anyone. Tell them how you feel – not what they should be doing.

Just as it may take years for you to break free from your negative communication patterns, it will take time for your family, friends and colleagues to accept the changes they find in you. But don't give up, because when you find a more sincere and genuine way to communicate with others your influence will help them to become more assertive – just like you.

Now that you understand more about the way we can express ourselves to get our message across, the next chapter will focus on particular ways we can send our message when we need to make a presentation. You may think that being yourself is probably the most unlikely way to make a successful presentation, but in fact that's what will make it enjoyable and interesting, and able to hold people's attention.

5
Presentation Skills

Most people dread the idea of presenting themselves in public, but, if you think about it, this is what we are doing every day. Whenever you leave your front door you are showing yourself to the outside world. So, how you look, sound and act is being viewed by other people. When you look at this way, making a public presentation is in some ways not so frightening.

In Chapter 1 I talked about the importance of being yourself, and this also applies when you're making a presentation. I have trained hundreds of people over the years and helped them to improve their presentation skills, and I believe the secret of their success is because I have given them 'permission' to be themselves. As I have said throughout this book, the only way to communicate effectively with others is to be yourself, not to try to use a persona that you think is appropriate for a particular situation. So, forget 'presenter mode' and work on managing your message by being yourself.

LOST IN THE DARK

The reason people don't like the idea of standing up in public is because it makes them feel vulnerable and exposed. Many of us have witnessed the amateur speaker perspiring, with a glazed look in their eyes, as they frantically try to remember the next part of their speech. What is actually happening in those situations is that they are so self-conscious and concerned about forgetting their words that they have memorised every part and are reading it out like a shopping list without thinking about what they are saying. Then, because there is no connection or meaning to the content, they lose their place and go into that horrible black hole where they can't remember their lines – and have probably forgotten their name and why they are there in the first place as well. I think a good description for this is the 'out-of-body experience'!

BE PREPARED

When you are presenting yourself in any situation you need first to go back to basics and prepare carefully. At some level you should have personalised your presentation or your speech so that it is *you* talking to your audience rather than a cardboard cut-out. The people who appear to make presentations look a breeze are the ones who have spent a great deal of preparation time on their content. You are never going to reach your full potential unless you have thoroughly prepared and researched the particular presentation you are doing.

Case Study: Richard

Richard was a very experienced radio and television presenter who confessed to me that having done speeches and presentations for years and successfully 'winged' them all, he had one recent terrifying experience that had left him feeling pretty shaken. He had turned up to talk about his given subject matter, and, true to form, he had not really put in much preparation – well, after all, he was in the media! And for the first time in his life he suffered terrible performance nerves that crept up on him from nowhere. He described how he simply went blank and couldn't remember what he was meant to be talking about. It made him go cold recollecting the experience, and even though his wife said that nobody would have known, he subsequently lost his confidence; so much so that he was now suffering from some inner anxiety even at meetings with colleagues.

I suggested he went back to basics and identified who he was going to be talking to (even if it was a small meeting as opposed to an auditorium), planned his message with that particular audience in mind and made sure he focused totally during his delivery. I told him to write some bullet points on a card so that if he did have a momentary lapse he had some kind of prompt.

Make use of your past

I feel qualified to pass on tips and advice because I have usually managed to make all the mistakes myself in the past. One of my greatest learning curves has been being the interviewee rather than the interviewer. The areas I found surprisingly difficult to begin with were so obvious but I hadn't even considered them. For example, I hadn't thought to include my own personal stories and anecdotes to support a point I was trying to make. After all, the best storytellers and comics often use their own case histories for material. Ideas come from other ideas and can be recycled.

I run training sessions with many authors who have to be interviewed by the media or give talks about their books. If they have not spoken in public before they are usually very nervous until I point out to them that the audience wants to hear about their life and what inspired them to write the book. So, we go back through their life together and they realise that they have a library of extraordinary material that will help them meaningfully illustrate the points they want to make. I remember one particular training session with a very interesting man who had become a well-known mountaineer. He was an absolute natural for public speaking but just didn't realise it. By the time we had finished our session he went away feeling much more confident, and since then I have seen him interviewed on various programmes, and he is now a major speaker. I know that the reason for his success is because he was given permission to be himself in a broadcast or presentation situation. Please take it from me, your life and experiences are of interest to others, you simply have to go back and review your own personal history, and be yourself.

So, when you are looking for material start with you. Go back through your life and look for the relevant experiences or stories that might help with your speech or presentation. Just remembering them will form part of your mental filing cabinet, and you've always got them at the front of your mind (as opposed to the back of your mind) if you need some filler material. You are going to give more authority and credence to something you have either experienced or have sound knowledge about. Blagging it simply doesn't work! There is a fine line between 'faking it to make it' and totally making it up.

....

Exercise: jogging your memory for anecdotes from the past

1 Your life events can be interesting to others and lighten up your presentation, so it's worth thinking about this in advance so that you have some stories to hand. To bring these ideas to the front of your mind, imagine you're describing yourself and your past to someone else.

2 Now think about specific anecdotes that might be relevant to a point you will be making in your presentation; for example, a world-class athlete giving a talk might refer to a sporting childhood memory, such as winning their first race at sports day and how it made them feel. Make sure the stories are brief.

3 Make a note of them in your presentation notes or just hold them in your mind – like a mental filing cabinet.

IDENTIFY YOUR AUDIENCE

When you are thinking about your audience you need to be clear about why you are there. Have you been invited? Did you invite yourself, or are you there to give your expert opinion on a subject? Identifying these issues will help you to plan what you're going to say. You need to consider the following:

1 Who are you talking to?

2 What do you want to tell them?

3 How will you keep them listening?

Although it might seem obvious, thinking about your audience is one of the basic factors that many people over-look. You can't your tailor your script or presentation if you haven't thought about who is going to be in the audience, because a good presentation is about making your talk relevant. One rule for all occasions won't work, so think about the following:

1 The age and gender of the audience.

2 Will they have any knowledge of the subject matter?

3 What are your aims? What do you hope the audience will go away with?

4 Do they need handouts?

5 Will there be follow-up sessions?

6 Is there contact information available?

Don't overlook anything; leaving these considerations to the day itself could be too late. Think about how you can make your talk informative, engaging, interesting and fun (if appropriate). Humour is a great ice-breaker. Consider too how you can involve your audience; practical sessions can help a group to gel and can produce some interesting results. Audience participation can be a real winner.

I was giving a lecture to a group of medical students about how to make a good presentation to the general public and I repeatedly tried to impress on them the importance of keeping their language simple and jargon-free. I pointed out that many of the people they would be addressing would be nervous about hospitals and illness, so it was all the more important not to use language that would scare them. I thought I had done a reasonable job until one medic stood up and announced that she could not possibly avoid medical jargon because her professor might be listening! This is an important point: if she had been thinking about the audience we were just describing, it would be highly unlikely that her professor would be included in it.

This can be a common problem with being a specialist, however, because it can be hard to dissociate yourself from your colleagues and profession and try to identify with the audience you are going to be talking to. But it is essential to consider that audience so that you can target your message clearly and give them information to make informed choices. There is no chance of an audience being able to do that if you haven't given them the full facts or you have used so much technical language that they don't know what you are talking about. Avoid language that will make you appear like a lofty intellectual. Acting in a seemingly clever or superior way will never win you votes, but naturalness and humour will.

Taking an active part

I remember giving a talk to a diverse group of people in the media about how they could raise their profile. They then divided into groups and I was fascinated and delighted by how much the groups got from each other. One young woman had been trying to work out why she had failed at the last three interviews she had been for. As the session came to an end she said that she realised from working with another person in the group that she had been going for the wrong kind of job. Solution.

This can be such an empowering and fulfilling way to work, and one certainly worth considering if you can bring it into your talk or presentation.

Talking at the right level

Once you are clear about who you are going to be addressing, your speech or presentation will start to form naturally. Are they children, young adults, all men or all women, or is the audience going to be general? As soon as you have identified the listener, it will make the job of preparing your talk so much easier. If they are interested in a particular aspect of your work, you need to write your presentation around that, but it is important to remember that even if you are talking to an audience of experts they are not going to be expert in every single aspect of the subject you are covering. Many people are frightened of talking down to, or patronising, the listener, but what often happens is the opposite: part of the audience isn't completely clear what you are talking about. In fact, a person in the audience can end up feeling more than just slightly in the dark; they can start questioning their own lack of knowledge, simply because you have made an assumption or used jargon they don't understand. What will then probably happen is that they will disconnect from what you are saying by pondering over something they didn't fully understand, and then you will lose them. Once they are lost, they may never return to the thread of the presentation. You have to use every tool you have to keep the audience hooked in from start to finish.

DRESS CODE

Once you have identified your audience and your subject matter you need to decide what would be the most appropriate clothes to wear for that occasion. Making a good first impression includes how we look. A dress code tells you what to wear for a particular occasion, and it will usually be written on invitations. Here are the dress-code classifications:

- ◀)) Formal
- ◀)) Semi-formal
- ◀)) Informal
- ◀)) Smart casual
- ◀)) Business casual
- ◀)) Active attire

You can find out exactly what clothing is appropriate for each of these codes by looking them up on the Internet. Put simply, though, what you wear will depend on how formal or informal the occasion is, but you will always be told beforehand if you need to dress for a formal occasion. For most presentations you will dress according to the situation, so if you are holding a presentation for a company or for a group of people on a training session, a business suit would be appropriate, or at least smart trousers, or skirt, and a jacket. If you are running a workshop for students, perhaps smart jeans or casual clothes would be appropriate. You want to feel relaxed and for your audience to be the same, although you must always look clean and tidy to create a good impression.

When deciding on what you intend to wear, also be aware that dress code can be led by religious or cultural influences.

The key point to remember is to explore fully the event you are attending and check the dress code with the organiser. You don't need the added pressure of turning up to give your talk and realising you look completely out of place with your audience because you are wearing the wrong attire. What we wear is a signal we send out to people. Make sure you send out a positive one.

THE PROBLEM OF FAMILIARITY

Remember Richard from the beginning of the chapter? Don't be caught out because you think you know your subject or audience well enough to manage without preparing beforehand. You should always prepare for a presentation of any kind, so that when the time comes to give your talk you are confident that you will keep your audience engaged from start to finish.

CONTENT

When making your presentation, don't assume your audience knows all the details without you telling them. If the story runs from A to Z, you have to fill in the bits in between.

Journalists can fall into this trap when reporting on follow-ups to stories: they give the viewer or listener only half the information, because they assume it will be remembered from the time before.

Don't let your presentation be like many conferences or seminars where everyone sits around nodding sagely and trying to look as though they know about the given subject matter, until one brave person puts their hand up and admits they haven't a clue about what's going on. It's not until then that everyone else breathes a sigh of relief and dares to ask questions too.

So, fill in the missing blanks. If you are worried that you might be talking down to people who already know this information, phrase it in a way that you are comfortable with. Here are some ways you could try:

'I know many of you know this already, but . . .'
'Just to remind ourselves . . .'
'Do you remember the time when . . . ?'
'I think this clearly illustrates the point I want to make . . .'

A good presentation is about going back to basics. This is usually where most poor presentations fall down. They make the assumption that some aspect of the information they ought to be covering is so obvious that there is no point in saying it. But it just leaves people wandering and getting lost.

Also, don't be tempted to try impressing your colleagues rather than addressing the crowd. It is far better to give a clear and well-focused talk that the audience can grasp. That in itself is the best PR exercise you can do for yourself.

Give it a lift

If you find your subject matter is a little dry, giving some real-life examples can make it interesting. Your talk or presentation is a story, and you need to make it engaging for you and your audience. Remember, it has to be interesting for you, otherwise, if you are bored by what you are going to say, there is not much hope for people on the receiving end.

Case Study: Sophie

I struck up a conversation with Sophie in an airport terminal. She was working on a speech she had to give to a group of musicians. She confessed to feeling nervous and was worrying about what to talk about to these fellow experts. Her main concern was that they would know everything already. Not true. People have specialisms, and however clever individuals like to think they are, nobody knows everything there is to know about a particular subject. As a teacher, she was perfectly comfortable standing in front of classrooms of pupils every day, even when she had not necessarily prepared the lesson in detail, but she felt very apprehensive at the thought of addressing colleagues.

As we were boarding the plane, I gave her some basic tips. I suggested she thought more closely about the audience she was going to be talking to and to look for subject matters that they would be interested in, then to consider how she might illustrate particular points she wanted to make. I also said it was best to keep it simple and not to make assumptions that they knew it all even before she had given her talk. During the flight she started to write down some stories and anecdotes, and by the time I met her in the arrivals lounge at the other end, she was positively animated about her forthcoming speech and relishing the idea of talking to these people. She had even come up with some practical examples she could use, and she recognised that her audience, despite their expertise, would not necessarily know everything she did about her specialist subject.

As Sophie left, feeling grateful and relieved, I realised that all her fears had diminished once she had been 'given permission' to be herself and to go back to basics. If you don't build the foundation stones properly you will have a potentially crumbling building. It's really all about the building blocks being in place and having the confidence to be you.

....

Exercise: break up your text with real-life examples

Earlier on we jogged our memories about stories from our life that might be useful in our presentations. Here we are going to look at it from a different angle: by looking at the text to see where it could be getting a bit heavy and could do with lightening up.

1 Any kind of presentation that is stuffed full of facts and figures becomes hard to digest for the listener and they can get information overload. So read through your presentation notes to find those places where you are giving dense amounts of information or facts.

2 Now see whether you can introduce a short story to illustrate a point. Or even a little joke to make it a bit lighter.

3 The simplest things can hold the most power, so go for brief and simple stories; you will keep your audience engaged, they will warm to you and they are more likely to remember your message.

....

KEEP IT CONVERSATIONAL

....

If you need to write something down, remember your presentation is the spoken word and not the written word.

And this really matters. So many people either don't know how, or can't bring themselves, to write their script conversationally. But it will sound better and read better if you do. If you write formal language for a speech or presentation, you're going to find it will make for uncomfortable reading and it will sound stilted and jarring. Here are some pointers:

- ◀)) Write short sentences and don't be frightened to use plenty of full stops, as these will help you with the pauses that give catch-up time for your audience.

- ◀)) Avoid sub-clauses, because they don't read well.

- ◀)) Don't use jargon or technical words that few people will understand. You really don't want to leave your audience with any question marks, or you will lose them completely.

- ◀)) Remember: less is more, and the key point above all else is to keep it simple. The cleaner and simpler your script, the better chance you have of giving it a good delivery.

DELIVERY

Although words and language are powerful, if your delivery is poor they will sound hollow. Without emotion and meaning behind them nobody will really get the message. It doesn't matter how good your content is, if your delivery is flat and dull your speech won't be a success. Remember:

1 Be connected to what you're saying and your audience will be there with you.

2 Be engaged – your audience will be too.

3 Be enthusiastic about what you're saying, because enthusiasm is infectious.

4 Use pauses and silence. Don't fill every available breathing space with words.

SILENCE

How many times have you felt the need to say something when everyone in the room has gone quiet? It's generally accepted that many of us are frightened of silence. Individuals holding presentations or speeches face the same problem: they try to fill every second, and that's a disaster for delivery. Let your speech breathe, and give yourself and your listeners a chance to catch up, or you'll lose your audience. More importantly, the message will start to manage you instead of the other way round. You will find that you speed up and are likely to gabble and disconnect from what you are saying. A pause or silence is literally a breath mark for you and your audience. It gives them time to assimilate the information you are giving them, to laugh or gasp – depending on what you have said – and it will make your overall delivery far more relaxed and natural.

PUT ON A GREAT SHOW

Don't be scared of putting your own unique stamp on your talk. After all, it is your presentation, and if you are interested you are going to come over as more enthusiastic – and that is going to help wow the audience. Just like the art of being a good storyteller, it's not only about the content, it's the way you tell it. People will enjoy your ability to 'tell' them in your own inimitable style. Whether you are presenting to one person or a hundred you have to ensure that each listener feels as though you are talking to him or her personally. Hook them in from start to finish. The number-one rule when you are presenting yourself in any situation is to be you.

ACT NATURALLY

As you know by now, acting naturally is the main theme of this book, but I can't stress enough that the very best presenters are those who can be themselves in front of an audience. Perhaps it would be more accurate to say, however, that they *act* more of themselves. It's back to the paint palette analogy I used in Chapter 1. Use the whole range of colours in your palette but give it that extra 50 per cent, just as an actor would on stage. You have to imagine that you are on the racetrack giving it your all, rather than just jogging around the park. The adrenalin you have will help you to give your performance that added colour and energy, which will be transmitted to the audience.

IF ALL ELSE FAILS

If you get into trouble during your presentation, use your humour to get you through. I had an unfortunate experience when giving a talk about how to use your voice to a group of parents and teachers at a school. My session followed one given by a top-class chef, who had wowed everyone with his soufflés and allowed them all a taste of his culinary delights. Then it was my turn, and right in the middle of the session my recording equipment went on the blink and I had to blag my way through the rest of the talk. Ironically, by making a joke about it and being honest I got the audience on my side and they apparently went away feeling they had learned something (albeit not on the technical side!).

I find myself reassuring broadcasting presenters that it is not the mistake that matters, it is the way we recover from it. Humans are fallible; if you stumble or say the wrong thing but you take it in your stride, you'll have a very forgiving audience. They'll forgive you for being human – in fact it is often a vote winner.

MANAGING THE MESSAGE

When you feel worried, you need to remember that you are the person with the information, knowledge and expertise. You need to manage the message and not allow the message to manage you. When the message starts to manage you, it's usually because you have concerns about what the audience will think of you, but that is usually a projection of your own self-doubt and fear. Experiencing some apprehension and nerves is healthy. It motivates us to achieve our best and not to be complacent. What's more important is how we use the boost of adrenalin that goes with it. A runner uses it to harness their energy on the starting grid – they channel and focus it and bring it into the moment. In the same way, we need to use that pre-presentation nervous energy to the best advantage. Take some good deep breaths, feel the ground beneath your feet and use that energy to help you focus and give a powerful delivery using all those colours in your paint palette.

You need to feel confident that you have done everything you can to give the best possible performance. I have a motto, which is: 'Every day I do my best. And some days are better than others!' We cannot do more than our best, and every performance is part of the learning curve and process towards improving.

When you successfully engage an audience they will warm towards you and relate to you. Those presenters who have the ability to make everyone feel at home and seem genuinely interested in what you have to say are usually bright, successful individuals who don't need to prove anything to anybody. The more natural we are the easier it is for our audience to engage with us. That is when we are managing the message. There is nothing worse than listening to a presentation where the presenter is sweating with nerves and stumbling over their words, or, just as badly, being patronising and aloof. But this is what happens when the message takes over.

My bête noir is to go to a smart ceremony where no expense has been spared on the venue and the lavish fittings, but then I have to sit and listen to a very inadequate speaker who fumbles their way through the script with no sense of connectedness. Be honest and be real. Manage your message and the audience will love you for it.

ON THE DAY

Once you find yourself up on the podium or stage it's important to centre yourself before you start talking. However difficult and false it may seem, take a breath, smile and try to engage with the audience sitting in front of you. Take some deep breaths and imagine you have roots going through your feet deep into the ground, the way you learned for the breathing exercise at the beginning of Your Paint Palette on page 18. This will bring you back to earth and help you to feel rooted and grounded. If you don't centre yourself at the start, you are going to rush into your presentation and lose your delivery and your audience. Although

RELAX – DON'T DRIVE OUT OF THE SKID

Nerves can get the better of you. It's a bit like when your car hits black ice. You are tempted to drive out of the skid, when actually you are meant to drive *into* it. When your nerves are jangling it will not feel natural to look relaxed and smile at everyone, but when you do just that, you will find it helps you to feel calm, focused and ready to deliver your words of wisdom (which, of course, you have prepared earlier and put into your mental filing cabinet).

it might not necessarily feel natural to begin slower, it will give you extra time and space, and that will benefit your presentation.

Having planned your beginning, middle and end (with some spare thoughts up your sleeve, just in case), take your time and focus on what you are saying. Your delivery will be far more natural and engaging if you are actually thinking about your content, and it will make your expression and intonation more natural.

Think of your talk or presentation in terms of a story with paragraphs. As you lead your audience through the tale you need to give them clues as to where you are taking them. It's what I call signposting and gear-changing. As you move from one subject to another make it clear, through your verbal and non-verbal gestures, what is going on. You don't want to lose your audience, so give them time to assimilate what you are saying as you go along, and they will be able to keep up with you.

YOU'RE TELLING A STORY

One of the exercises I give journalists and non-broadcasters is to get them to practise reading through a news bulletin. I find this an effective training method because they have to read a selection of completely different stories and somehow bring the audience along with them using delivery and pausing to show that they are moving to a different story (known as signposting or gear-changing). So, for example, they read a tragedy, which has to sound sad, but they might then have to move onto a business story, which needs to sound businesslike. The final story might be some good news, which needs optimism to be reflected in the voice and delivery. Your speech or presentation works in the same way: it is like a story with different aspects to it. The natural meaning will be reflected in your delivery because you are connected to what you are saying. This will ensure that the audience stays with you while understanding and assimilating what you are telling them.

The structure

It is good to have a general introduction to the presentation, then let the audience know what is on your agenda. For your conclusion, sum up the key points you have made, and perhaps mention any follow-up sessions you may be running, or have that handout ready so that they go away with reminders and, of course, your contact details.

EYE CONTACT AND BODY LANGUAGE

Open body language and good eye contact is important because it instils confidence in your audience. If you know your subject and believe in what you are saying, that will be transmitted to the people you are talking to and will come across naturally in your body language. I don't think you can fake body language. As we all know, someone can say something and not mean a word of it, but the truth will be in their gestures and their eyes. Closed gestures, such as crossed arms and a lack of eye contact, are giveaways. Remember to engage your audience with eye contact as described on page 62 and with relaxed but confident body language (see pages 63–4).

PRESENTATION FEARS

People have all kinds of anxieties about making presentations, and they're not all to do with the fear of standing in front of hundreds of people. It's hardly surprising, though, when you consider that statistics claim a fear of public speaking ranks second to people's fear of dying!

Case Study: Maria

I took a coaching session with Maria who was a successful manager in charge of a finance department in a large corporate organisation. She had a proven track record and had survived numerous staff cutbacks. She was popular and had good team and leadership skills and she really knew her stuff. Every couple of months Maria had to give an audit account to her colleagues, and every month she was filled with trepidation, yet when we analysed the situation she didn't really have anything to be nervous about. She had the respect of her colleagues, she knew her facts and figures, and she had a great track record; she also had good management and communication skills. When we analysed the situation we realised that the only part of the equation that was unfamiliar was the setting. It was held in a conference room, and we deduced that the only thing she could be nervous about was the furniture! The rest of it she was doing on a daily basis anyway, with the support and backing of her colleagues. Being able to talk it through and have a bit of a laugh helped diffuse her nerves and take control of the situation.

Although many people have a genuine fear of presenting in front of large groups of people, for some it is the opposite problem: they are comfortable with addressing a crowd but hold back more in social situations or in meetings. In other words, they will speak up only when asked or given permission to do so.

Case Study: Gerry

I worked with Gerry, a manager of a large IT department. He was well liked and considered to be very good at his job. He was more than capable of standing up in front of crowds of people and delivering well-honed speeches. In fact, he enjoyed them and always got good feedback. Ironically, though, his boss thought he was too quiet in meetings and sometimes reluctant to offer his valuable advice. When we had our session, Gerry admitted that he found it hard to start conversations with people he didn't know. He also confessed to not liking the sound of his own voice, which in my experience is a common problem. Our goal was that he should find ways to give himself permission to speak up. We set targets, including joining in a conversation, even if he didn't really want to, rather than someone else asking him to. So, he moved from being the attentive listener to someone who could initiate conversations, break into them and offer his thoughts. He practised his new skills at dinner parties, forums and seminars and said that it boosted his confidence as well as enhancing the way he communicated.

Whatever your fear, be assured that you can overcome it. Work through this book to help you relax and enjoy the experience rather than being held in a grip of fear.

YOUR PERFORMANCE CHECKLIST

Run through this list to check you are ready to go:

1 Identify your audience.

2 Target your message.

3 Prepare, and don't try to 'wing' your presentation, whether it is in front of one person or a hundred. If you fail to prepare, you prepare to fail.

4 Have key messages and use simple language.

5 Think about your dress code.

6 Remember you are in charge of your message.

7 Breathe and centre before you start.

8 Engage with your audience.

9 Stay connected and keep the audience with you.

10 Remember, it's not just what you say but it is also how you say it.

11 Leave plenty of room for audience catch-up and reaction time.

12 Use confident body language and good eye contact; it will get you a long way.

Most of all, enjoy your performance. If you do, it is almost a guaranteed certainty your audience will, and remember:

> By being yourself it makes it safe for others to be themselves.

There are other times in our lives when, whether we like it or not, we need to be able to present ourselves in a good and confident way, and that is when we are interviewed. In the next chapter I'm going to help you prepare yourself for a variety of interview situations including radio and television.

6
Interview Skills

For most of us the word 'interview' means applying for a job or a place at university, but there are other situations where you might find yourself being interviewed: by a journalist for a newspaper or magazine, or by a presenter on the radio or television. Of course, you may also work, or plan to work, in the media, so knowing what to expect and how to deal with different situations as they arise is valuable. This chapter covers a wide range of interviews using the experience I have gained over the years of working in the media and training others to feel confident when speaking.

Interviews are an opportunity to show how good you are, whether applying for a job or talking about something you know. But on the other hand you can completely let yourself down. It all depends on your interview skills. Most people let themselves down when they are being interviewed because of one of the following two reasons: 1) they have not prepared properly; or 2) they let their nerves get the better of them. In this chapter I am going to show you how to plan and prepare for any type of interview and succeed.

MISTAKES: OUR VALUED TEACHERS

One of the reasons I became a voice and communication coach is because of my own personal and professional experiences. People tell me that my training is realistic. I think that is because I can identify with anyone trying to progress and do well at home or at work. The road we travel is never straight, with many bends on the way, but we make the greatest improvements when we learn from our mistakes. Let me share with you the worst interview I have ever done – it was a huge learning curve:

Many years ago I went for my first broadcast job interview. It was at a commercial radio station in Glasgow and the programme controller was notoriously terrifying. Relying on my reasonable interpersonal skills, I went totally unprepared. After the niceties, this tough Glaswegian started asking me about the city's football teams, population statistics and various wide-ranging questions that I didn't know the answer to. It was a very humiliating experience and I went away with my head literally in my hands.

A few days later, the programme controller very kindly wrote to me listing all the questions I had got wrong and inserting the correct answers. I think you can probably imagine how that made me feel, but I did recognise that I should have researched the area properly and done my homework. Some months later a job opportunity arose at the sister radio station in Edinburgh. Well, I hardly need to tell you how much preparation I did for that interview. Suffice to say I turned up knowing every street name in the city and, of course, I was not asked a single question about the area! But, guess what – I got the job! I duly wrote a letter to the other programme controller and said I appreciated his feedback and thanked him for his advice, which I had taken on board and I had now secured a job at the sister radio station. I am sure that must have been rather a mixed blessing for him.

Only make the mistake once (or twice)

Lack of preparation or believing you can wing it is something I think most of us will do at least once in our professional lifetime. A friend of mine who was a very experienced television producer turned up for an interview for a job on a national magazine programme believing the position was already his. He had not done enough research and the interview bombed. Embarrassing.

The point is, whatever happens in life I believe we can see it as an opportunity to learn and grow. But I hope the general tips and specific interview situations in this chapter will help you prepare and give the best interview possible whatever the circumstances.

KNOW YOURSELF

The first place to start is by reviewing your own curriculum vitae. Look at your past experiences and how they might benefit your current situation or the job you are going for. Don't make the assumption that your prospective or current employer will know all about you and remember everything you wrote on your job application. We have to take personal responsibility in every situation for selling ourselves, so prepare yourself by remembering all the qualities and experience you have to offer.

If we overlook the basics, we are in danger of leaving out critical information that could win us that contract, promotion or pay rise. Apart from anything else it is a good idea to review your past successes regularly. Not only is it good for your self-esteem but it can also be useful in terms of letting other people know your strengths and capabilities.

I find I look back at my life and experiences at seminal moments like a big '0' birthday or when one of my children has reached a particular age or stage. Every time I do it I am genuinely surprised at how my life has slotted together like a jigsaw puzzle. I feel a sense of achievement when I remember some of the difficult times I have come through and my triumphs over adversity. On those occasions I can also see that some of the events I perceived to be negative at the time actually turned out to be very positive, because they sent me in a different direction – the right direction. These events are like signposts in our lives. See your CV as a road map, which you can use to illustrate your talents and abilities.

Keep up to date

I'm not suggesting that you turn up at an interview and spout off your exam grades. It's more about being up to date in your head, and if you have recently reviewed your CV, it will be fresh in your mind so that you can give coherent examples and illustrate points you want to make with interesting stories.

Case Study: Jenny

I remember coaching Jenny, an accountant, who found herself in the unfortunate position of having to attend board meetings where the other participants had misogynistic attitudes. Every month she dreaded spouting out the audit accounts. She felt preoccupied with self-doubt and also admitted she was bored by her own material. I suggested she tried to think of ways to illuminate the facts and figures and to put them in an interesting context. We discussed different ways in which she could present the material, and as we looked back over her past achievements she felt much more confident and inspired. She later told me that reviewing her own CV had been one of the most useful exercises she had done in her long career.

When you look through what you have done in your life – and it is useful to go back to the beginning – you will find that all those extra-curricular activities you enjoyed could provide material for your interview; for example, perhaps you were a volunteer, or you have travelled to extraordinary places, or you were given an award or participated in extreme sports. Those experiences reveal aspects of yourself and attributes that will serve you in the workplace. They are all part of your USP.

UNIVERSITY AND COLLEGE INTERVIEWS

Young people need to be helped with their interview skills, because these days it is not just your academic achievements that will win you that coveted university or college place, it's what you can contribute as an individual to university life. Your social and emotional intelligence are factors that interviewers will take into account, as well as how you engage with others and what good personality traits you have – such as showing initiative and leadership skills. The competition is high and the interviewers will be looking for individuals who have that something extra. Ask yourself what makes you stand out from the crowd. What do you have that they might want?

Any college or university is keen to accept students who will help them to raise their profile. The key thing to remember is that interviewers may be impressed by some of the attributes or achievements you are inclined to dismiss, so look back through your CV to remind yourself of them.

ARE YOU BLIND TO YOUR POTENTIAL?

In my coaching sessions I often see someone else's potential when they are blinded to it. Coaching provides feedback that helps people build on positive aspects about themselves. As humans we are not totally self-sufficient, and so we need feedback and compliments from those around us. It gives us interconnectedness, which is one of the joys of being human.

Case Study: Jackie

Jackie, a presenter, had been suffering a crisis of confidence despite her years of experience. During my first coaching session I gave her lots of reasons why she should feel positive about her career and future, and we looked at how she could help herself. Shortly afterwards, we had a follow-up session and she told me how much everything had improved in her life since we had worked together, then she repeated back to me the advice I had given her. I could not believe I had said all those helpful things to her, and I realised that I needed to hear this feedback just as much as I needed to give it out!

Why an interview is valuable

It's difficult to sell your personality on paper alone, but further-education establishments today place a great deal of emphasis on emotional intelligence; in other words, they want to know how motivated you are to achieve a degree, how you interact with others and what your interpersonal skills are like. These aspects of yourself are best projected during an interview, so it's important to prepare yourself to make the most of all your personal qualities.

Be prepared

Give yourself the best possible chance by planning ahead for your interview:

- ◀)) Make sure you're clear about the basics, such as where you are going for the interview and what time you need to be there. Give yourself plenty of time and aim to be early.

- ◀)) Think about what to wear. Going dressed as a typical student might not be the way to get a place.

- ◀)) Think through possible questions the interviewer might ask you, and practise your answers in front of friends or family. Your school or sixth-form college should have a general idea of the kinds of questions you might be asked. Remember to be honest with your answers.

- ◀)) Flag up your strengths but be aware of your weaknesses. To be able to admit there are areas you need to improve on will impress your interviewer and will show that you are taking personal responsibility, which is a sign of maturity. One of the key areas they will be interested in knowing about you is how you will structure your time around lectures and get your work done without the supervision you might have been used to having at school and/or at home.

- ◀)) Read up about the university or college you want to go to, so that you can ask them questions about anything you're not clear about.

HARD WORK WILL WIN THROUGH

Places are sometimes given to enthusiastic and hardworking students who have not achieved the grades they wanted, but you will need to prove you are one of these by the way you respond in your interview.

Exercise: remembering your achievements for an interview

1 Don't be afraid to let your interviewer know about your interests and past achievements, so think about these before the interview.

2 Have you done any voluntary work, been involved in the Prince's Trust, worked in a hotel or shop or dealt with the public? These are all worth using as examples of how well rounded you are as a person.

3 Have you ever been sponsored in a charity event? If you have taken part in sponsored walks for charity it shows you have physical stamina as well as having an altruistic side to your character.

4 Do you have any particular interests, such as amateur dramatics, or do you belong to a sports club or exercise regularly?

5 Make a list of all these qualities and experiences.

JOB INTERVIEWS

When you receive an invitation to be interviewed, you have already passed a selection process and have been chosen above other people to be there, so the organisation will be seeing you as a potential employee, with the interview as the deciding factor. Many companies now operate a points system for applicants, where you have to reach a certain score to work for them, so don't leave it to chance – prepare as much as you can.

Think about your USP. An interview is your chance to sell yourself, but be selective about what you are going to offer this particular organisation. You may have many talents, but you need to consider which ones are right for the job you are going for.

Make sure you know about the company's competitors and its owners, and any general industry and market information. Find out what you can about the position you are seeking within that organisation and what will be expected of you. Make a note of anything you can't find to ask about on the day.

Fact Statistics have revealed that 85 per cent of people who go for an interview are dismissed as potential employees within the first five minutes because of their lack of interview skills.

Aim for that perfect interview

Here are some hints to help win over your interviewer:

- Dress appropriately. Think about the job you are applying for and dress accordingly. Don't wear anything that will divert the attention of the interviewer in a negative way. Remember to look clean and tidy and dress so that you don't stand out; for example, avoid ties with ludicrous designs. For most job interviews, play safe by wearing a suit, shirt and tie, and avoid plunging necklines or loud jewellery, because you want the interviewer to concentrate on you and not on what you're wearing or not wearing.

◀)) Don't be late. Being late for a job interview is unforgivable, so leave in plenty of time. It's always better to have time to spare so that you can be calm and centred before your appointment.

◀)) Use positive body language. That means: good eye contact, a smile and a confident handshake.

◀)) Be fully prepared and bring an extra copy of your CV. Get your mental filing cabinet in order so that you have some questions to ask the interviewer. This shows initiative.

◀)) Be focused all through the interview. If there's a panel of people interviewing you, make sure you have good eye contact with all of them. Listen carefully to their questions and take a breath before answering so that you are clear and confident. Be factual and keep your answers relevant, giving examples where appropriate. Be honest about your strengths and weaknesses.

◀)) Sell yourself. You don't have to be pushy to sell yourself, but you want the interviewer to feel you will be a real asset to their company.

◀)) Enquire about the next stage. Ask what happens next, but don't mention salary or bonuses until they do.

◀)) Before you go shake your interviewer's hand and thank them with a smile.

PROMOTIONAL INTERVIEWS

If you are applying for promotion within the company you work for, don't rely on having friends in the department or a good track record to ensure your success. As mentioned under Job Interviews, many organisations today use a points system, and at the interview they will want to see how you perform.

Make sure you prepare thoroughly and haven't assumed that your interviewer will know or remember all the wonderful things you have done for the company in the past. It is your responsibility to ensure they know how good you are and to flag up your USP. Go back over your CV and your work record, and find examples, statistics and testimonials to prove your worth.

POST-REDUNDANCY – STARTING AGAIN

Redundancy is not just about losing a job; it's a kind of bereavement. You are leaving a place of work, your colleagues and friends when you had planned to stay there. It can lead to feelings of personal rejection, sadness, anger and even despair. Going through this 'bereavement' period, however, is an important part of the process of change. It's important to allow yourself some recovery time, but what you decide to do has to be your own decision. You might choose to go on holiday with your family and have a month off before going back into the workplace, to give yourself time to reflect on what you want to do. Rushing into the next available job might not be best, but financial considerations will obviously play a part in dictating your next move.

If you don't grieve or fully experience your sense of loss you will not have closure, and ultimately you will find that it is difficult to move on. Give yourself some time to come to terms with the changes that you and your family will have to make. You may find, as I have, that the darkest and most difficult times will bring the most positive changes. Allow the process to work at its own pace – be patient and steadfast. If you possibly can, take at least a few days off to think about your skills and your next step.

Taking it personally

One of the acknowledged reactions that people who have been made redundant experience is the blow to their self-esteem. Even if the situation at your company was completely beyond your control, being made redundant can still feel extremely personal. During times like this it is important to seek outside support and help. Find out about counselling services near you, or find yourself a business coach or mentor who can help you plan for the future.

Set goals

When you feel ready it's time to plan your next move. Change might be frightening, but it's also liberating. If you have been made redundant, you now have a clean slate before you, so start by looking at what you would like to do in the future, not just what you think you *should* do; go with the flow and you are more likely to succeed. Perhaps you will even find that you can move in the direction of your dreams.

Firstly, sit down and work out what you would like to do and what you definitely don't want to do. If there were aspects of your former job that you disliked, it's pointless applying for a similar position. Instead, look around to see what kinds of occupations might suit your skills, and remember that it's important to go for something you will enjoy; the happier and more content we are, the more productive we will be in the workplace. Also, think about whether to train for something completely different. During your search you might even discover a new and exciting profession that you had never considered before.

Embrace life's opportunities

Try to keep a clear vision of what you want for the long term, but be open to opportunities that arise along the way; for example, many years ago I found myself signing up for various facilitation and coaching courses while I was working as a crime reporter in a television newsroom. I felt inspired to do the courses but never imagined at the time that they would serve as an integral part of my work. It was probably a decade later that I became a trainer and coach, and was able to put to good use the skills I had learned all those years before.

Case Study: Caroline

Caroline trained as an interior designer and had a successful business in London. After her two children were born and her husband lost his job she became a childminder, because it fitted in with her life at that time. Eventually, however, she returned to her original career, but when her marriage broke down she found she couldn't continue with that, so left work and took in lodgers.

At the age of 52, Caroline then found herself working on the tills in a large DIY store as this was the most appropriate work for her present circumstances. Not only was this a culture shock but she also found herself on the receiving end of some passive-aggressive behaviour from the boss, who thought she was too educated for the position. He asked her to arrange a social evening – presumably he was expecting her to fail. But Caroline organised such a successful night out that her boss found respect for her and never bullied her again. For Caroline all these experiences helped to build up her self-esteem and confidence, and she is now a successful art gallery owner. She puts her current triumphs down to all the various working experiences she had in the past.

You don't have to give up on your dreams but you do have to be prepared to follow the winding road and take opportunities along the way that will help you to build a better portfolio. Today, multi-skilling is the key to finding a good balance in the workplace. A job for life no longer exists, so the more skills you have and the more adaptable you are, the more likely you are to be successful and to create some stability for yourself.

Go with the flow

When applying for jobs, don't be put off by interviews that come to nothing; no interview or application is wasted – you will learn from every experience. Be honest with yourself and others about your redundancy – but don't let it make you feel a lesser person. Because of the recent economic changes more people have found themselves out of work, but it is nothing to be ashamed about. It's a good idea to be clear and communicative about it from the outset, but to feel able to move on.

Your USP

Every one of us has at least one unique selling point that will single us out from the crowd, but many of the people I have worked with fail to recognise their own talents. We admire other people, without recognising that what we see in them is often a reflection of our own abilities. The trouble is that the things we find easy are the things we overlook, because we tend to focus on what we cannot do as well. In the past people were encouraged to try to be good at the things they found difficult, but surely it is better to perfect our own gifts and qualities. I believe that we are born with innate talents and abilities, and it is important to do the things that inspire us. And these can embrace a wide spectrum. Find what drives you. Most highly successful people will tell you that it is not just the money that motivates them but the excitement and risk of a new venture. I worked with a woman recently who set up a coaching venture and as soon as things were in place she announced that she was ready to start a new project. Job done, as far she was concerned.

Don't let age stand in your way

One of the problems that an ageing population faces in the workplace is ageism. But when you are looking for employment it is important to remember the benefits that being older and wiser bring, and promote those in a job interview. You can bring mentoring skills to the workplace as well as years of experience – and that's not just experience in business but also in life. If you have brought up children and worked in various industries over the years, that shows you are adaptable. Being older means you are more self-aware, understanding, tolerant and experienced. The key is to be prepared for any interview and to be yourself, then see how your natural abilities will help you to get that job.

Bringing it all together

If you are looking for a new job or a new direction after redundancy use this checklist to help you:

◄)) Identify your skills and update your CV.

- ◀)) Find out what your USP is.

- ◀)) What are your strengths and weaknesses? Do you need extra training?

- ◀)) Ask for advice from the experts – that is what they are there for.

- ◀)) Research your options, and if you are going for an interview, make sure you know about the company and identify the areas where you can benefit them.

- ◀)) Even if you don't succeed at that first interview, try and try again. It's all good experience, and if you persevere you will get there in the end.

MEDIA INTERVIEWS

I thought it would be useful to include how to deal with an interview with the media in this chapter, because media organisations are more reliant than ever before on the public helping them with their newsgathering process.

Do you have a story that the media might be interested in? It could be a life experience or a book you have written, or some charity work you have been involved in. Your first step would be deciding who your audience would be, and then you need to consider which medium would be the most appropriate. If you want your story to appear in a magazine or newspaper, you will need to be interviewed. Another option, if you already have some media experience, would be to produce your own broadcast-quality story. If you have some interesting footage that you can offer a television station, it will be extra enticement for them to use your story.

Perhaps you have a story that you think is so exciting that it would be an 'exclusive'. You will need to decide which media organisation you are going to target first. Whichever route you decide on, remember that this is your opportunity for free publicity, which is useful if you are, for example, talking about a book you have written or you're announcing a large fundraising event for your community.

MEDIA OPPORTUNITIES

If you hear a story on the national news and you feel that you, as an individual or company, can give a reaction, then contact your local newspaper, radio or television station. Journalists and broadcasters are always happy to be given stories, as it helps to fill their pages and airtime.

When you're invited to comment

You may find you are contacted by a journalist because they want to interview you about a particular story. Your role might be as a representative of a group of people or a company for a newsworthy item. There are a few things to be careful about. Do your fact-finding before you answer any questions. Ask the journalist:

1 Which company do they work for?

2 What is their deadline?

3 How can you help them?

4 Who else have they spoken to and what information do they already have?

5 Establish the time, location and venue where the interview will take place.

Content

Make sure that you have prepared your message in advance, so that everything is at your fingertips for the interview when it takes place. Think of the content in terms of an inverted pyramid with the most important points first and then the detail following. Order your thoughts by using the headings: who, what, where, when, why and how. Keep your message simple so that it will be easier for the audience to understand.

Interviews in print

Use this checklist to get ready for an interview that will be published in a newspaper or magazine:

1 Research the newspaper or magazine you are being interviewed for.

2 Plan your message.

3 Make sure it's *your* story that is published, not the story they want it to be.

4 Don't give yes or no answers to any question put to you by the reporter, or your one-syllable response could become your quote.

5 Never say anything is 'off the record', because it may well end up in print.

6 Make sure that what you say is balanced and fair. Don't say anything that could result in a lawsuit. If you have an opinion, preface it with 'I' or 'in my experience' or 'in my opinion'.

7 Keep a note of everything you have said, just in case there's any comeback. If you say something that you are

subsequently not happy about, tell the reporter before it goes to print. Journalists will not let you see what they have written before it is published, but they will not deliberately put in anything factually inaccurate, because it doesn't show them up in a good light.

8 The more helpful, informed and friendly you are the more likely you are to be become a good contact for the journalist who interviewed you.

Radio interviews

If you are being interviewed on the radio there are several things to do beforehand so that you are fully prepared and relaxed. Firstly, find out whether the interview is live, pre-recorded or by telephone. Is it on location or in the studio?

Never launch into any 'on air' interview without knowing who is going to be interviewing you. If you have been contacted by the radio station, find out beforehand what questions they will be asking, and exactly what the piece is about. You will need to keep it succinct, because although you may be an expert in a particular field, the listeners won't want to hear an A to Z of your specialist subject but just one or two particular points. Find out as much as you can beforehand and be well prepared.

The urgent interview

Although journalists always have deadlines, don't feel pushed into doing an interview instantly. It is professional and acceptable to find out what they are going to ask you, and then you can call them back in ten minutes. This means you can go through your who, what, where, when, why and how list, and ensure that you have some good soundbites prepared. Make sure you are in control of the message from the outset.

THOSE DIFFICULT QUESTIONS

It's critical to be able to consider in advance any hostile or unwanted questions that may come to you. If, for example, you know there is something that you may be asked that you would rather avoid, it's no good just hoping it will not come up; you need to prepare a get-out clause. It's never a good idea to be defensive or rude. All that will do is put you in a bad light and even make you appear culpable when you're not.

In my media training sessions many people have been more concerned about what they don't want to say than what they do. Don't waste energy worrying about the negative, but use this airtime as a great opportunity to promote yourself. If, for example, there has been some bad publicity in the past about your organisation, and you are inevitably asked about that, don't get defensive or deny it. Acknowledging the question and turning it to your advantage is the key. So, for example, you could say:

'Yes, that was a difficult time for the company, but we learned many valuable lessons and I believe that is why I am sitting here with this success story today ...'

If you are asked questions that you cannot answer, don't try to deceive them. Be honest and say that it is not your area of expertise, but tell them instead what you can comment on. Acknowledge the question and move on to talk about something you are confident with.

Don't forget the nitty-gritty

In the past I took part in a number of publicity interviews for books I had written. I had researched all my material and knew what the publisher wanted to me say, so I had lots of interesting facts and figures ready. But in those early days I had not given enough thought or consideration to my personal life, so I struggled with questions about myself. So with all interviews, never overlook the basics. Review your CV as well as anything relevant from the past, to gather together any useful source material.

Getting on with the interviewer

The success of any interview will often be down to the rapport you create with the interviewer. Even though you are talking on radio rather than television, your body language and eye contact is critical. If you look defensive, or if you are aggressive in your verbal or non-verbal communication, you won't give the best interview.

In the interview

Now that you are fully prepared, get ready to be interviewed. Here are some points to help you:

- ◀)) Keep your language simple, listen to the questions and allow a pause for editing purposes and for you to gather your thoughts before you answer. This helps you to manage your message.

- ◀)) If you're worried you might leave out a critical point, take a small card with some bullet points into the interview with you. Don't take in wads of paper; they might confuse you and, worse still, they will produce terrible paper-rustling sounds.

- ◀)) Breathe properly, talk slower and stay connected to what you are saying. If you rush, you will disconnect with your message, then you will find that you are not listening to the questions properly, or you'll get caught in self-criticism in your head, which will distract you from what you want to say.

◀)) You know your story better than anyone else, so don't worry about a lack of knowledge.

Television interviews

Many people have a fear of being interviewed because they feel they cannot be themselves, but the best interviews are those with people who are well informed and *natural.* In the same way as radio interviewing, know what you want to say and also be prepared for the questions you might not want to be asked, by using them as an opportunity to promote you or your business. See the list above for interview hints.

Studio

If you are being interviewed in the studio, although the setting may be unfamiliar, just remember that you are talking to that one person (the interviewer) and don't become distracted by anything else going on around you. This is your chance to shine, so don't let anyone or anything get in the way.

Clothes

Do think carefully about what to wear. The setting and reason for the interview will to a certain degree dictate what is appropriate, but there are some basic rules that revolve around what works on camera and what doesn't.

◀)) Check the setting of the interview. If the television studio has particular colours, it is worth thinking about how your outfit will blend in.

◀)) Check if there is any particular colour that will not work on set.

◀)) Avoid wearing all white or all black. White can glare and black can make you look as though you are disappearing into a hole.

◀)) Don't wear patterns that will strobe, such as dots or thin stripes.

◀)) Don't advertise your logo or be blatant about any form of advertising.

◀)) Take a change of clothes in case something is inappropriate. You don't want to have a crisis of confidence when you are told to wear someone else's shirt or jacket.

Getting ready for the interview

Before you are taken into the studio you may be taken to the 'green room', which is a hospitality suite. Remember that you have to take responsibility for your personal appearance in both senses of the word; for example, if you are not taken to the make-up department, make sure you have checked your make-up, hair and clothes. In my experience, presenters and camera crew are not great at letting you know if something looks horribly out of place. They are usually too busy worrying about their script or technical stuff.

There will be other guests in the green room as well, which can help with the nerves. When you are taken to the studio, regardless of whether it's an 'as live' situation (which is recorded but not edited, so appears as a 'live' interview) or a 'live' interview, you need to be just as focused and connected to what you are saying.

◀)) Answer clearly and thoughtfully, and be yourself.

◀)) Listen to the interviewer and any other people who might be on the programme with you. You may well want to react to something they have said, so be alert.

◀)) Don't talk over the top of the presenter or other guests.

◀)) Be confident enough to correct anything you are not happy with.

◀)) Emphasise anything you feel strongly about.

◀)) Watch your language and body language.

◀)) It's better to avoid them having to retake the interview, as that can undermine your confidence.

Remote studio

A remote studio is usually a very small studio setting with a chair and camera (or microphone, if it is for a radio studio) and just you. The interviewer will be in a different location. Although this can feel unnatural, make sure that you are completely focused on what you want to say. Listen to the questions carefully and give yourself plenty of time to answer.

PULLING FACES

Whether you are with other guests in the television studio or in a remote studio, be aware that the camera could be on you at any time, so you don't want to be seen doing something you would rather the viewing public didn't see. Think about your facial expression; most people who are inexperienced in interviews get caught looking glum or scared, because they don't realise the camera is on them. If you are taking part in an interview that's not of a deeply serious nature, do smile when the interviewer mentions your name. Remember that you are on show from the minute you walk into that broadcast arena until you leave it.

The telephone interview

This is the type of interview that can catch people out. It can seem less limiting in the sense that you are talking to someone on the other end of a phone so you may feel a little more relaxed, but as a result you might find that you are less in control of what you are saying. On the other hand a telephone interview might seem unnerving because you are talking to someone you cannot see. Both reactions will affect your message if you allow your mind to slip from what you are doing. Be extra vigilant and aware of the points you want to say, and stay focused from start to finish.

KEY POINTS FOR MEDIA INTERVIEWS

1 Be proactive as well as reactive.

2 Check if it is pre-recorded or live.

3 Find out the location (think about what you are wearing).

4 Identify your audience.

5 Plan your message, including your soundbites.

THE INTERVIEW ITSELF

1   Be relaxed and calm – smile, if appropriate.

2   Talk slower.

3   Stay focused and connected.

4   Avoid fiddling with things such as pens, as it will distract the viewer.

5   Don't be defensive – acknowledge the question.

6   Avoid using any jargon.

7   Keep it simple so that the viewer instantly understands what you are saying and does not mentally wander off.

8   Use useful bridging phrases such as: 'I would like to emphasise ...', 'The key point I am making is ...'

9   Keep the viewer hooked in and manage your message.

10 Give examples and anecdotes. It's always better to back up your message with an example.

11 If you make a mistake, go back and do it again or clarify it. It is OK to correct something on air, but instead of saying, 'I have made a terrible mistake ...', say something like, 'Let me make that point again ...', or, 'To be clear ...'

12 Deflect unwanted questions by acknowledging them, but then say something that you do want to include.

13 Enjoy it, as this is your chance for personal promotion, and make sure you get your message across.

Dealing with hostile interviews

Hard as it probably is, try not to take a hostile interview personally. The interviewer is only doing what they should be: finding out answers to questions. If you are representing yourself or the company you work for and the interview is about a subject that has stirred up some controversy, you are bound to be asked some tricky questions.

For many years I trained police officers in interviewing techniques and they were, usually without exception, bitter about their negative media experiences, and blamed the journalists for having asked them 'difficult' questions. I can honestly say, however, that there was not one situation they described that couldn't have been avoided if they had prepared for the inevitable hostile enquiry. The important thing is to rehearse your get-out clauses. Here are a couple of ideas:

'I'm afraid I'm not in a position to answer that, but what I can tell you is . . .'
'That isn't an area I cover, but what I think is important in this situation is . . .'

POINTS TO REMEMBER

- ◀)) In any interview situation, ensure that you give out only the information that can be transmittable.

- ◀)) However stressed you may feel, don't swear or say anything you may regret later.

- ◀)) If you are covering a subject that is of public interest, point this out in the interview.

- If you don't agree with something but feel obligated to mention it, you can use phrases such as: 'I think some people might think ... but ...'

- Respond in the most positive way you can to the most negative questions, but don't ever lie, as you will be found out, especially in these times where accountability is a priority.

- If you do say something you are not happy about, put it right straight away. You will be forgiven for being human but you will not be forgiven for lying.

- Be cautious in a contentious situation, and, rather than admitting guilt on air, you could say something like: 'Right now we are doing all we can for the [*family/ employees*], but we will be carrying out an investigation so that this doesn't happen again.'

- Don't try to blag your way through anything. It's better to admit that you don't know the answer but will let them know as soon as you have one.

- Set the record straight. If an interviewer has got the facts wrong, don't be defensive, but put them right. You could use a phrase such as 'Yes, a lot of people think that, but the truth is ...'

Make any situation work for you

On one particular occasion I was being interviewed live by a television presenter about a book I had written. The producer had told me that the presenter was a 'pussycat', but she was more like a tigress in my experience. She tore into me and repeated the same question over and over again when she didn't get the answer she wanted. It could all have gone badly wrong, except I realised I was being given a fantastic opportunity to capitalise on the airtime and to take the interview in the direction I wanted. So each time a hostile question was flung at me, I politely acknowledged it and then said what I wanted to say. I was able about to talk about the publisher's viewpoint and my own personal experiences, and I could convey the message I wanted to rather than being at the mercy of that obnoxious presenter. Afterwards, the feedback I got was that I had been engaging and interesting, and by being centred and calm I had got my message across clearly, but I am not sure the presenter came out in such a good light!

BEING A GOOD PRESENTER

Although we have been talking in this chapter about being interviewed, some of you may work in the media or be thinking of working as a presenter. The exercise I am about to give you is one I have suggested to a wide range of people, from health professionals to teachers, to help them understand what makes a good presenter. It's all about studying how other people work.

What is it about someone's delivery that makes you listen or not? The answer to this lies in analysing it from the viewer's or listener's standpoint. You, as a viewer or listener, probably like some presenters but dislike others, so finding out exactly what you like or dislike about them will help you to tailor your own style to be a good presenter (this can also help if you're planning to be interviewed). When I watch the television or listen to the radio I form a first impression: do I understand what's being said? Has the story left me with question marks?

Did the narrator keep me listening, or did I get distracted? Now try the exercise.

Exercise: what makes a good presenter?

1 Start watching and listening to the news in a more conscious way.

2 What are your first impressions?

3 Does the presenter look or sound as if they are interested in what they are telling you?

4 Do they have a sing-song delivery or a glazed look at the camera?

5 Are they engaged with the listener or viewer?

6 Does the interviewer listen to what their guests/ interviewees are saying and then respond to the information they are given?

7 Use your responses to the points above to clarify what you want to aim for or avoid.

GETTING THE MOST OUT OF INTERVIEWS

Any interview is about being yourself and convincing your audience, or prospective employer, that you are the best person for the job or that you come over as a credible interviewee. If you are not asked the question you expect or want, it is still your responsibility to get your information over, and a good interviewer will pick up on this and ask you the right questions to draw out those points.

Interviews are not something to be endured, but a great opportunity for you to promote yourself, because only you can do that, so it's worth doing well.

In the next chapter we are going to look further into promoting yourself through the media and networking. There are many times when we might need to sell ourselves, and I'll show you how to get the best out of raising your profile without feeling difficult or uncomfortable.

7
Raising Your Profile

This chapter is all about raising your profile through networking and using the media, and these are avenues that anyone who wants to promote themselves or their products should consider using. Whether you have written a book, painted a picture, conducted some research, want to raise sponsorship to help someone in need, or you want to promote your own business, there are some simple and effective steps you can take to get yourself and your message out there. In truth, most of us baulk at the idea of having to sell ourselves, but we are going to explore how you can be seen and heard in a way that you feel comfortable with.

Having a vision, or clear goals, and a focused sense of direction is critical to your success:

'A vision of where you want to go and who you want to be is the greatest asset you have.' (anon.)

I'll be explaining how we can do this.

WHO NEEDS TO PROMOTE THEMSELVES?

We all need to be able to promote our skills and abilities, particularly in the workplace, but we often find it hard to do this. We feel it might come across as being arrogant or boasting, but if we are to get the career we seek, or win important work for our company, it's essential that we know how to do this.

Being able to promote yourself is primarily about self-knowledge and self-belief, because your efforts will not be successful if you are trying to convince someone else of your worth when underneath you don't really believe it yourself. It's understandable, though, that most people are reluctant to get out into the market place and sell their wares. It's so much easier to do that on behalf of someone else and more challenging if you are selling yourself.

WE CAN ALL BENEFIT FROM REVIEWING OUR SKILLS

I ran a Raising Your Profile seminar for lawyers – professionals who would not necessarily see marketing as part of their role. I have found that people in this profession naturally shy away from promoting their specialisms, seeing that as the preserve of another department. I started off the session by suggesting that they probably didn't know how good their own skills were and that they had probably not thought about reviewing their curriculum vitae for a long time. What's more, I suggested that they might not be up to date with their business partners' current expertise either. To prove the point, and to allay their scepticism, I asked the group to divide into pairs and to spend some minutes in a fact-finding exercise where they would talk to each other about their skills and experience. Knowing about each other's credentials would mean that they would be better equipped to network on behalf of their colleagues (and therefore their firm) as well as themselves. The results were illuminating. All the people at the seminar were surprised at how little they knew about each other's work and how essential those up-to-date pieces of information actually were; for example, if a lawyer had switched to working with defendants rather than claimants in court it would be a vital factor if the company was recommending their work to someone outside.

KNOW HOW GOOD YOU ARE

Not only did the lawyers in my seminar discover they had little knowledge about their colleagues, but the next exercise, which involved looking at their own CVs, was to prove even more revealing. All of them, without exception, discovered that they had forgotten how many high-profile cases they had covered over the years and how much expertise they could offer their clients.

Although I have used the example of lawyers here, what I have to say applies to anyone in any profession. We need to keep track of our past and be up to date with our recent successes as well as looking towards our future goals. Not only can it boost our self-confidence but it is also a vital asset when it comes to networking. If you don't know how good you are, you are going to find it difficult to promote yourself with any kind of inner self-confidence. The problem is that as we go through life, we gain more workplace and worldly experience but we forget our earlier achievements along the way, because we are so caught up in the moment or looking for the next opportunity. Often, we assume that the person we're trying to impress already knows how great we are, but we can't afford to take this risk, and very often the fact is that they don't know, or don't remember, as much as we think they do.

Gaining inner confidence

It can give us a great deal of inner confidence to go back through our work history and review our achievements. And when we have that inner confidence we will radiate an aura of success. Of course, by this I don't mean a strutting arrogance, but more a sense of being comfortable with who we are and what we can offer.

During my session with the lawyers I acknowledged that they were probably self-effacing and would prefer to look at their clients' cases rather than their own achievements. However, I persuaded them that a personal review could prove helpful to them, if only to serve as a reminder of how experienced and competent they were.

NETWORKING

For this particular group I held follow-up sessions on an individual basis, and compiled a set of targets, which were designed to help them raise their profile through internal or external networking or capitalising on their media opportunities. We then reviewed these targets after a few months to help them keep on track. They acknowledged that the work we did together had helped them recognise their own worth, which made networking and promotional opportunities easier. Interestingly, they then set up monthly internal meetings so that they could pass on information to other lawyers in the firm as well as keeping them updated on any changes.

Why networking is important in the workplace

We're inclined to think that networking refers to finding contacts outside our place of work, but networking inside work is vital too. Remind yourself regularly of your own talents and abilities and of those around you, so that you and your colleagues are better equipped to advertise on each other's behalf.

Using networking to find opportunities

The word 'networking' essentially means getting out there and letting people know what you can offer them, and most of it is directed outside the workplace. Unfortunately, the very idea of networking fills many people with horror, and they shy away from it, but it's really very simple; it's about letting people know what your latest venture is or offering something that may be helpful to them.

To network effectively you need to identify what you have that other people might want. So we are back to our theme of identifying your audience and targeting your message. In other words, which individuals or groups of people would benefit from your skills or services, or your product?

As always, once you bring it back to basics the whole idea of networking is less daunting and more practical and possible. Let everyone know about your new business or product. Word of mouth is without doubt the best (and, of course, the cheapest) form of advertising.

How networking can help you

Networking can be very profitable for your business and can help you to generate new clients, but you'll only get the best results if you are prepared to put some energy into it and to follow up the leads that people give you. Although I understand people's ambivalence about networking, because they don't want to seem pushy or a nuisance by following up an initial contact, you have to realise that if you don't reconnect with your contact your competitor will.

Target the right people

To get results you need to target the people who are going to be useful for your business or what you want to achieve. I have become slightly exasperated by a colour-photocopier salesman who insists on ringing and emailing me months after we met at a business fair. My recollection of events is that I told him I didn't want an industrial-sized photocopier. But that wasn't what he wanted to hear, so every so often I get this overly enthusiastic call telling me about the latest great offer on a high-tech laser printer that is designed for a corporate company rather than a one-man band!

This example illustrates that you have to be discerning and clear about your market and how you are going to target it. Equally importantly, you need to communicate with your potential customer or client in a way that leads them to respond favourably towards you.

Remember, it's a journey

There are such a large number of networking business and social events available that the choice is almost intimidating. But you need to turn up to as many as possible, because it is important to find out what works for you and what doesn't.

I have been to more business breakfasts than I care to mention, and one of the things I found was that there is often a very competitive element to recruiting new members. I was pleased and flattered when one woman enthusiastically invited me to her particular networking group, which had local traders and small businesses as members. I dutifully turned up at some unearthly hour and forced down some scrambled egg while various traders stood up and extolled the virtues of their wall tiles, carpets or latest gadget. Then all the members had to pronounce publicly how many people they had referred on to other businesses during that week. I found it very intense and quite scary. More importantly, I was not convinced that my voice coaching would be of any interest to the florist or the body builder. Furthermore, I was disappointed when the friendly woman who had invited me walked past me in the street after I had said that I didn't think the networking group was for me.

Learn through the process

The art of networking is a process. You will meet people you have something in common with only if you look for them, and that is not necessarily going to happen instantly. Nevertheless, our rewards can come from our willingness to do what it takes to get out there, and the more energy we put into something the greater the returns will be.

What we do have to help us on our networking search is the Internet, which is quite incredible in terms of what it can offer. Put in any question and you will be overwhelmed by the information that will come back. I think the key here is not to be daunted by the choices you are given but to just narrow them down.

It's not a one-way road

Of course, networking is not just one-way traffic. In the same way that you hope your contacts will extol your virtues to those they are in contact with, so must you reciprocate. I believe I am a natural networker for others (although perhaps not quite as good for myself), and if you are genuine in your referrals you will probably find that you get them in return. The more interest you show in someone else and their work the more likely they are to reciprocate. You will, of course, experience times when you feel that you are outside your comfort zone, but the more courage you have to get out there and find your voice, the easier you will eventually find it and the bigger your rewards will be.

I appreciate that the idea of networking and putting it into practice is not always easy, and some people find it more difficult than others. There are times when even the most experienced public speaker or sales person probably feels that they would rather stay at home than get onto the podium and sell their stuff. Whenever I have experienced those moments, however, I have felt doubly rewarded for my efforts after I have finished. Usually the meeting or networking event has turned out to be far more enjoyable or lucrative than I could have imagined, and, apart from anything else, I have met interesting people and learned something new.

In a networking event you have to approach people you have never met before, and that's bound to be a little nerve-wracking for many of us. But if you feel apprehensive about going up to a stranger, remember that is how many people feel, so just rise to the challenge – you may be surprised by what happens.

Don't just do it cold

In the last chapter, on presentation, I explained the importance of thorough preparation. You need to adopt a similar routine for any networking you decide to do. Here are some ideas:

1 Think about the venue for the event you are going to and the people you are likely to meet. Research the networking organisation.

2 Come up with some key points that you would like to make.

3 Be fully prepared to answer any questions about your product or business, as you want to be able to come across as being yourself as well as being well informed and aware of your target market.

Social networking on the Internet

Many people are using social networking websites for building up their businesses and just keeping in touch with others. You will find local business sites, sites for women in business, professional sites and, of course, Facebook and Twitter. These sites are constantly evolving as well as coming in and going out of fashion, but there's no doubt that such sites can benefit you. If you're working as a freelance or have your own business, they can be a way of making links with others. If you're an artist or writer you can upload pictures of your current work onto your networking site. The opportunities are endless, but you need to see how they can work for you – the best way is to join one.

Personal recommendation

Many people would say that their best work comes to them through personal recommendation. This has certainly been the case for me. Recently, I was at a meeting of professional corporate coaches and one man said that he had advertised extensively through all sections of the media and had had a paltry three replies. Reputation counts for so much, and I know that I have always received new work through references from other people. One thing I have found very helpful is to ask for testimonials when I have completed work for an individual or organisation, because coming up with an impressive list of clients' positive feedback is a sure way to get new work.

We have looked at how you can improve your general networking skills and now we are going to explore the many media opportunities that are around.

THE MEDIA

First of all, don't be intimidated by the media. Journalists have this terrible reputation for being intimidating, but I have to say that, being a journalist, I think this is rather unfair. It is like saying that all police officers are corrupt, all lawyers only want your money and all politicians are dishonest. Across all sections of society you will find people who abide by the rules and those who do not, so there will always be some journalists who bend the rules, but most of them don't. Journalists are basically messengers, and they can be a great benefit to people who have a story to tell. If you are using the media, as long as you remain in control of the message you are putting out, you have nothing to fear. For the purposes of this book I will cover aspects of the media that you can use to promote yourself, your business or your product.

News media

The news media is the general term used to cover all aspects of current news that are available to the public; in other words, news items as they happen, not just on a daily basis but hour by hour and minute by minute. The rapidly changing face of technology means that the speed at which we can receive information is instantly transmissible.

Once upon a time journalists were the messengers of news, but technological advances, including mobile phones, have meant that news organisations are becoming more dependent on the public providing them with stories. So in this ever-changing environment, it is no longer about journalists digging about to find front-page stories but more about individuals and organisations coming to them.

NEWS IN ALL SHAPES AND SIZES

There are different types of media, both traditional and modern:

◀)) The print media: newspapers (published daily, weekly, biweekly, monthly, bimonthly, or quarterly), news magazines, magazines, periodicals, trade publications.

◀)) The broadcast media – radio and television.

◀)) The Internet.

The changing media

The advent of online journalism has truly changed the face of the news media as we know it. This has partly arisen because financial problems in the traditional news outlets have caused journalists to turn to the Internet instead. Apart from BBC television and radio, many news outlets use advertising, but this has reduced over the years, mostly because of competition by the Internet. Today, we also have blogging, which means that anyone, anywhere, can write whatever they want and publish it on the Web. This can draw in a potentially massive audience. The Internet is now considered to be a leading source for news, and younger people, particularly, look there first for any information they might be seeking, news or otherwise.

Don't be daunted by these changes, but know how to embrace them and make them work for you. Change is inevitable, and if we don't go with the flow, we will become stuck and be overtaken.

Managing the message

You want the public to know about you or your product or services, so the media is ideally placed to help you. But don't be concerned that the media will work against you; instead, think of it as a team player – after all, it needs you as much as you need it.

As I mentioned in Chapter 6, I have trained many police officers over the years to help them work more effectively with the media. At the start of practically every session, I had to break down the inherent barrier that exists between the police and journalists. The truth of the matter is that most police officers are scared that they will be exploited and have their message distorted, and they feel that they are altogether at the mercy of the journalist. But this is not true. It is in a journalist's interest to take a good interview and have a good story, and that will largely depend on the interviewee.

Helping a journalist to help you

Journalists do not have the time to redo inarticulate interviews or to edit an incomprehensible answer to get it ready to go on air. They want the person they interview to be clear and to give them a strong story. Promoting yourself well can mean you become a regular contact for a journalist; for example, I knew a woman who was a PR officer for a major organisation but she made a point of becoming a regular guest on local TV and radio. Because the journalists knew she would be a good interviewee, she was often called in to comment on a range of subjects.

When working with the police, a journalist obviously wants a good story that is going to make the headlines or the top of the radio and television bulletin, but the police also benefit because the publicity means they are more likely to get help from the public in solving the crime. It works both ways. So, the media can be a useful friend rather than an enemy to be avoided at all costs.

There was a time when the media was glamorised as a profession but people viewed journalists with suspicion. Today, the public are becoming more involved with journalists and the media generally, creating their own news stories, and even filming footage on their mobile phones.

Making the most of the situation

Journalists give the public information so that they can make informed choices. Their stories are gathered from various sources, many of which, as I have already said, come from the public. It is important, then, to adopt a proactive approach to using the media. This is where you might find an opportunity to promote yourself or your business as well as helping out the journalist by giving them a good story or feature. The general public will be able to find out about you this way and it's a great way to attract new clients.

REAL LIFE BEYOND CELEBRITIES

Because today we live in a celebrity culture, there is underlying pressure, especially on young people, that we have to look and behave like celebrities if we want to be successful. This makes it difficult for us to speak with confidence and self-assurance, because we feel we probably don't meet an acceptable standard. Don't fall into this trap because you are using the media to promote yourself. It's being yourself that will make you successful, not trying to be something you are not.

How to target the media

Remember that journalists need your story as much as you need their publicity. The key point is that you need to give them something to write about. First of all look at the following factors:

- ◀)) Who is the audience you want to target?
- ◀)) What is the message you want to give them?

You might decide that the local paper is the best place for you to start, but if there is enough interest your story could be picked up by national papers and the broadcast media – even across the world. Sometimes material is shared between individuals and organisations: you might do an interview for a local BBC radio station and then find it on the national or even international news or the Web. But there is no doubt that every journalist wants their scoop, so you may well be able to provide them with one.

Here's a look at the different kinds of media:

Local newspapers Although primarily print-based, local newspapers are becoming more reliant on their website content and are also using video journalists. However, many people regularly buy their local paper, and prefer to read the local news this way. It's a good outlet to use for almost anything you want to advertise or promote about your achievements or a new venture.

National newspapers If you're thinking of approaching a national newspaper, first consider the political leaning of the paper you are choosing to target, as this will affect the position they take on any news story. Then think about what kind of stories they run and whether, or where, your idea would fit in. As I explained in Presentation Skills (Chapter 5), knowing your audience is essential when writing for a newspaper. The quality newspapers will have firm ideas about the style and content of writing.

The tabloids I think it is fair to say that the tabloid news-papers are a law unto themselves. They have a reputation for creating the ultimate headline news, as many individuals and organisations have found – sometimes to their cost.

Trade press This is a useful route to go down if you have a particular brand or product that a niche market would be interested in. Do your research first to ensure you are targeting the correct trade paper for your business.

Radio There are numerous commercial and public broad-cast local radio stations, not to mention network radio broadcasters, so you need to research them all. Make sure you know about each station's audience in terms of age, gender and interests.

Television With the advent of satellite and digital TV there is a wide choice of channels to choose from. You need to be aware that your material can be used by more than one of them. Once you have recorded your interview and given permission for it to be used on one programme it could also be used in other programmes, and even on other channels.

Internet This ever-expanding medium has transformed our lives in terms of instant and global communication. Websites such as MySpace and YouTube have changed the face of celebrity, fame and success. The wonderful thing about this kind of access is that if you have a good idea, millions of people across the world can read about it, see it or hear it, thanks to this international marketing tool.

Have you got a story for the media?

The more headline-grabbing your story is the higher the profile it will get. Obviously, regional papers will be looking at more locally based stories, which don't necessarily have to be sensational to get some print space. You have to identify the story element so that you can sell the idea to the journalist you are approaching.

There are lots of ways you can attract the attention of the press. Here's one example: if you run a company you could commission a survey or do some research, and if it produces some useful results, you might have a good news angle. When preparing your subject for the journalist, think about the human components in your story. Put yourself in the position of the reader, listener or viewer. What would interest you? Going back to these basics will help you compose your press release.

Press releases

There is always the temptation just to use product placement. This is usually where manufacturers of goods or providers of a service pay for their products to appear in films and television programmes, but it can also work where press releases repeatedly mention a company name and its product. No news organisation can flagrantly promote anyone's product, so I'm afraid that if you try this approach it's more likely to lead to your particular story ending up in the shredder.

A well-written press release is your key to getting your story out there to the public. Don't be daunted at the prospect of putting one together – it's the best way to get your story published. Journalists are under so much pressure that if you email a well-written story there's much more likelihood that it will end up in the newspaper or on air. As newsrooms become more financially squeezed and journalists become more multi-skilled (that is, filming and editing their own pieces), they are more likely to be grateful to receive a good story – but it has to be well composed and balanced.

Here are the elements that should go in:

1 Decide which part of your story would make a headline. How are you going to hook your audience in?

2 Think about who, what, where, when, why and how in relation to your product; they make up the key components of any journalist's story, so you will need to answer these in your press release.

3 Keep the language simple. Avoid jargon and technical terms that will leave your audience baffled. Remember, for a press release especially: less is more.

4 Use the pyramid technique: start with an overall headline statement that sums up your situation or story, and then go into the points of your story, prioritising them in such a way that if your words are cut down or edited you will still get your salient points across.

What makes a good press release?

Having a strong story line is essential, but if yours would not stand alone try to think how you or your product could be part of a larger picture. You want to reach as many people as possible, so make sure your press release is user-friendly and to the point, and that the news is relevant and topical.

Have some follow-up ideas or tie-ins you can offer. Ask yourself why a news editor or journalist would want to publish your story, and remember that the more work you do for them in preparing the words, the more likely your message is to get out there.

Going further

As well as giving the news organisation some good headline-making facts, make sure you are available for comment or interview, whether in print, or on radio or television. Be proactive and ready to be reactive to any other relevant story the reporter may be interested in. You can go one step further and arrange a possible photo-shoot or invite the press to an event that will give you the publicity you seek.

What's different about broadcasting?

In broadcasting it is the immediacy of the story that counts. If you want to get on the radio, however, think about the audio elements of the story. Who will be interviewed? Would sound effects be used? How will you paint a full picture?

If you are thinking of approaching a television company with an interesting item, there needs to be a strong visual element to your story with obvious pictures. Although graphics can do much to help a story along, a good television item is one that has excellent pictures, so you need to think about this before approaching any company.

Every journalist and news organisation loves an exclusive. If you have one, you can agree to sell it or give it exclusively to your chosen organisation, or you may want to give one medium the opportunity to publish or broadcast it first and then allow any other news medium to carry it afterwards.

WATCH OUT FOR THE PITFALLS

Many years ago, I agreed to give an interview to a tabloid newspaper about my experiences of living in an alternative community with my family. I was assured that it would focus only on the positive aspects and that several people would be interviewed. I had no reason to believe this would not be the case, particularly as I knew the journalist.

However, I broke all my own rules: I agreed to a telephone interview rather than being interviewed in person. What's more, I probably didn't think through my potential answers carefully enough, and I also allowed my young children to answer the reporter's questions, which were 'yes' and 'no' to whatever she said to them. I didn't see the article before it went to print and when I saw the skewed headline and the completely fabricated quotes I can safely say it was one of the most distressing experiences I have ever had in my professional career. I had no comeback, as I could not afford to take on the might of a tabloid owner.

I've mentioned this here because we are all fallible – even in our own particular profession. Although I continue to be a trusting person, I have most definitely learned through my own unfortunate experiences. I am, at least, able to console myself by being able to pass on these lessons in my media training sessions!

MEDIA INTERVIEWS: POINTS TO REMEMBER

- ◀)) Be proactive, but be prepared.

- ◀)) Know your audience.

- ◀)) Target your message for that audience (are you they young, older, interested in your subject matter?).

- ◀)) Be aware of the medium you are approaching. Know what their programme and bulletin deadlines are. Make sure you research the programme and the types of topics they cover. It will give you a better idea of how to produce the best story for them, or at the very least get them interested in talking to you.

- ◀)) Prepare for the interview, using Chapter 5.

Helen Boaden is head of news and current affairs for the BBC. Here, she gives a good picture of the direction the media is going in and how people can find their voice through using various media:

> Finding your own voice in our digital age has never been easier. Social networking, YouTube and blogging, to name but a few new ways of communicating, have given people from all walks of life the chance to talk about what matters to them and to be hugely creative with technology. Big news organisations increasingly use material supplied to them by ordinary members of the audience to enrich – and sometimes create – the main news stories. We've had phone-ins for years, and they are still a powerful way of hearing opinions from across the spectrum, but now emails, texts and user-generated audio and video coming from our audiences have transformed our access to what is going on in the world and what people think about it. Of course, we check everything out using old-fashioned journalistic checks and double checks, but this is a change in hearing the voice of our audiences – and it's unstoppable.

PUBLIC RELATIONS

Sometimes it's hard to sell our own story, and this is where a PR consultant comes in. A good PR consultant will enhance your image, and will also use their contacts book to your advantage.

So what is PR really about? Linda Donaldson runs her own company, Geometry PR. I think she gives some very sound advice here:

> The use of the term PR has become one of the most overused and least understood phrases commonly used in

our everyday language. Consider how often you or someone you know has said, 'We need some good PR,' or 'It's all just PR,' when referring to a newspaper article or a TV programme.

One important point I would like to put over first about PR is the notion of spin. Spin, thanks to the last ten years of government, has largely become associated with misrepresentation and perhaps a level of deceit. This somewhat grieves PR professionals, because what a PR professional will do is represent you in the best possible context.

Good PR is all about adding credibility to your marketing. PR is not about spin; it's about you, your reputation and maintaining a profile. PR is less to do with publicity stunts and more about raising your profile in a meaningful way that builds a positive reputation for your brand, product or yourself.

It's difficult to generalise about PR because there is no one-size-fits-all strategy. What works for one person (or company) won't necessarily work for another, even if they are operating in a similar sector with a similar product. But one thing I have learned from running a PR consultancy is that you have to be specific, strategic and focused to make your PR work well for you. Be deeply suspicious of any PR practitioner who comes to you with an instant solution or a generic product.

So what did I mean by strategic? It's important to take time to sit down and work out exactly the right message and your target audience. This is the basis for any PR strategy. In the same way that you write a business plan for your bank or a flatplan for a book, you start from objectives and work out how you are going to achieve them.

In PR speak, we talk in terms of: who is the audience, what is the message and how best to communicate it. Sounds simple? But you would be amazed at how difficult it sometimes is to achieve just that.

So Linda's message is the same as I have been discussing elsewhere in the book: be clear about your message – in this case what or who you want to promote – identify the people you want to reach and ensure that you get them to listen. I think that promoting oneself can be extremely difficult. I find it much easier to network for somebody else rather than myself, and I think that many other people may feel the same way. So, using an outside consultant can be helpful. The important thing is to ensure that you feel comfortable about the strategies they use and that they are in tune with you and your product. It's a good idea to go to someone who has been recommended to you rather than randomly selecting a name out of the phone directory or the Internet. So use your networking skills to ask around your contacts.

Why good PR is so important

On one occasion I held some training sessions for a large consultancy that was wasting some wonderful PR opportunities. Their PR department had generously invited the local media to some rugby and cricket matches over the years, but when I saw their invitations I expressed concern that they had not explained clearly enough what their company actually did. Sure enough, some months later, one of television news editors mentioned how much the newsroom staff enjoyed the freebies they were given, but nobody had any idea what the company's business was. That is clearly not good PR.

The lesson here is not to be frightened to get your message out there as clearly as possible, and, if necessary, to find someone who can help you to do that effectively.

To promote ourselves the way I have been explaining here requires us to be self-confident about being ourselves and, as I explained in Chapter 2, this comes from finding our personal voice – the part of us that is unique and makes us special. In the next chapter I look at how our complete lifestyle affects our personal voice and how we can work towards helping our voice become stronger.

8

Your Body, Your Voice

I n Chapter 2 I explained how discovering who we are and finding the confidence to be ourselves will affect our whole lives – this is our 'personal voice'. When you find that inner strength it makes it easier to believe in yourself rather than feeling insecure by comparing yourself to others. We then looked at the many practical ways to approach speaking, whether to one or two people or a crowd, always being ourselves, whatever the situation. But finding our true expression in life is not just down to one thing. In this chapter I'm going to explain how our whole body contributes to that feeling of self-confidence.

When we care about our body and our mind, every part of us benefits. So, we need to take a holistic, or whole-centred, approach to how we live. What we eat, what exercise we take, the homes we live in, the company we keep and the space we give ourselves for fun and enjoyment are all part of the journey of our life that makes each one of us different. We need to look at how we live and find ways to deal with those areas that are not in a healthy balance; for example, stress is a major part of our lives today, so finding ways to de-stress is essential, whether through meditation or exercise, or through our relationship with animals. I'll be covering all these areas, and including a practical exercise to help you support this personal aspect of your voice.

WHAT IS A WHOLE-PERSON APPROACH TO HEALTH?

Many health professionals now acknowledge that a whole-person approach is the key to a healthy body and life. A whole-person approach means looking after your health through diet and exercise, as well as learning how to relax and letting go of your worries to avoid the effects of stress. Finding our personal voice, and inner confidence, comes through taking care of ourselves physically and mentally, and finding an even work–life balance. There are many aspects to this, but one that can give us instantaneous results is exercise. It can be a great mind- and energy-booster, and revitalise us. I have found that swimming or dog walking, or just getting out and enjoying a change of scenery, can totally change how I am feeling. What's more, it's great for creativity. Some of the best ideas I have ever had have come to me when I am ploughing up and down a swimming pool or out walking. It seems that if we give our mind a rest, the creative ideas and inspiration can come through.

HOW DO WE FIND HEALTH AND WHOLENESS?

When we are ill, how interconnected are our physical symptoms to our mental, emotional and spiritual well-being? How strong is the link between how we choose to live our life and how we find our personal voice in life? I think there is a connection, because so often our physical bodies exhibit symptoms that link to how we are feeling or thinking; for example, a leg injury might symbolise that we are not able to move forward in our lives; throat problems could occur because we are not communicating our truth; and breathing or respiratory problems could be connected to us not feeling safe.

Do you feel that your life is out of balance? Often we get caught up in the stresses of life, and it's not until everything becomes unmanageable that we are forced to change. A crisis is often the catalyst for change, but if you know that your life is out of balance it is better to take action before the crisis happens.

Our individual circumstances affect our health. People may become ill if they are living where they are unhappy, or if they feel trapped in the wrong job or in the wrong relationship. If this is you, it's essential for your health and happiness to find ways to change those situations. They will stop you from living your personal truth – in other words, just being you – and that will stifle your personal voice. You can only find out what you truly want in life by giving yourself time to reflect and to plan your goals, and then start to live differently. Change is scary, but eventually it will be liberating and freeing.

Allow yourself 'you-time'

Set aside some time every day just for you. More and more people are recognising that finding 'you-time' is not being selfish, in fact if you don't take care of yourself in this way it will ultimately have a negative effect on everyone around you.

BALANCING YOUR FOCUS

How balanced do you think your life is? A useful way of finding out is to use the following simple but effective method, called the wheel of life. It helps you to see if you are focusing too much on one area of your life and ignoring another.

......

Exercise: the wheel of life

1 Draw a wheel and divide it into eight sections. Now label each one to represent an aspect of your life; for example: health and fitness; relationships; family and friends; career and work; finances; recreation; self-confidence and self-esteem; and personal development. (You can use any other labels you feel suitable.)

2 On a scale of 0 to 10, the centre of the wheel equals 0 and represents those aspects of your life that you feel are unfulfilled; the outer edge equals 10 and represents those aspects that are very fulfilled. Now, colour in or shade the various sections according to whether you feel the aspects of your life they represent are fulfilled or unfulfilled; for example, if you feel that you are fairly concerned about health and fitness, colour in half of that section.

3 Now look at the completed wheel. You might be quite surprised at the result. You should find it to be a good indicator of what is working for you and what is not. Those sections of the wheel that are not shaded in as 'fulfilled' need your attention.

4 Use this starting point to help you set goals and begin to address the imbalances in your life.

......

After about six weeks, go back and colour in another wheel with the same section labels, and see if things have progressed and improved. If they haven't progressed, you need to do something about them, as they can have a profound effect on your quality of life and your health.

TIME TO REFLECT

To improve the quality of your life you have to develop your inner awareness, which gives us space for thought and reflection, peacefulness and tranquillity, but we need to find a quiet mind to do this. Apparently we have over 60,000 thoughts racing through our minds every day, so stilling the inner chatter gives us an opportunity to access our deeper wisdom – our intuition and inner knowing (as explained in Chapter 1). You can either start practising a simple meditation or just focus on your breathing for 10 or 15 minutes – but make it a daily practice and you will begin to find your life really does change from the inside out.

The benefits of meditation

Meditation brings stillness to the mind, and this quiet time has beneficial effects for your whole body, improving your general health and well-being – and it can benefit your relationships too. The reason so many people advocate it is because it is a great way of de-stressing and calming the mind, and it also helps us to learn to tune out of the myriad thoughts constantly racing around our head. Meditation helps us to access another deeper part of ourselves and to learn to be more in touch with our innate wisdom and intuitive self. The most basic meditation is focusing on the breath.

Exercise: meditation

1 Choose a quiet place where you won't be interrupted. Sit on a chair or cross-legged on the floor, but make sure you are comfortable, whichever way you choose. Keep your back straight, to enable clear breathing (and to avoid the risk of going to sleep!).

2 Close your eyes, and start breathing naturally through your nose. Become aware of your breath going in and out.

3 As you concentrate on your breathing you will notice that all the other thoughts that are racing through your mind start to fade into the background until eventually you will find yourself in a new space of lucid awareness.

4 If you find that your mind is wandering, or you start following a particular thought, just bring yourself back to your breathing. Keep doing this until your mind naturally settles on the breath.

5 Continue with this meditation for 5 or 10 minutes.

6 Try to do this meditation every day, preferably at the same time. You can gradually build up the time to 20 minutes, if you like. You will soon start to notice that it has a positive impact on your life and you will feel less stressed and generally more relaxed and peaceful. Once you have mastered this breathing meditation, you can go on to explore other meditation techniques, which you can find in numerous books or on the Internet.

GOAL SETTING

For our lives to be meaningful and purposeful we need to have targets to aim for, otherwise our existence becomes meaningless. But we also have to ground them in reality, so before we can aim higher we have to find a route to get there. It makes more sense to work with our natural talents and abilities. Perhaps you could keep a journal where you record your thoughts and desires. Writing down your hopes or dreams is one way of starting to give voice to them, and the more we do that the more likely they are to happen. It's because they become part of an action, step or foundation stone for creating that reality, and you begin to work out in your mind how you can move forward.

YOUR WORK–LIFE BALANCE

Unfortunately, the 'stress' word is all too familiar these days, and it doesn't only occur in the workplace. If you are trying to juggle work with your family and social life you can easily feel overloaded, so it's important to try to find a balance between your work and home life that will help you feel better and be more happy and productive in both areas. Stress is also responsible for many illnesses.

Good health is not just about your physical body, in fact often the symptoms of physical illness are the external signs that you are suffering inside with stress-related or mental problems, and it's quite probable that is has taken months, or even years, for you to have become ill.

Beginning to create that balance

Emotional, mental and, for some people, spiritual well-being is critical to managing our stress levels and finding some kind of inner equilibrium. Getting back to basics will help with these emotional aspects as well as the more obvious physical ones. Ensure you eat well, take regular exercise and get enough sleep. And it is obviously good if you can avoid smoking and keep your alcohol intake within healthy limits.

Be serious about relaxation

One of the most important ways to create balance is taking time out to enjoy yourself and relax. But it can be hard to do, especially if you are feeling stressed and overloaded, because you will constantly feel that there is not enough time in the day and so you will cram more and more into it. The very last thing you feel you should be doing is relaxing. But ask any meditation practitioner and they will reinforce the notion that you need to look after the inside to benefit outside. Taking time to contemplate or just to 'be' and really enjoying what is going on in your life right now can be the most productive action you can take. By stopping, you allow the frantic chattering inside your head to quell, and then the creative and productive ideas can come in.

Work smartly

Get the most out of your working day without feeling crushed by the stress of it. Here are a few things to think about:

- ◀)) It's not necessarily the number of hours you put in but ensuring that the productivity levels you get out of them are good. You can probably do more in a shorter space of time if you're not feeling overloaded and tired, which will just make your brain feel scrambled. Learn to switch off when you're not working – turning off your phone or laptop can be a good way to start.

- ◀)) Manage your time. We all have different ways of doing this, because how we manage our time depends on our personality and characteristics, but there are a few ways that work for most of us: be focused about what it is you need to do, prioritise and try to keep things simple. What works for me is to allocate jobs into time frames, so, for example, once I know a deadline, I can create the space to do the job to meet that time frame. It doesn't necessarily follow that the more time you are given to complete a job the better it will be, because many of us work better under pressure when we have to meet a deadline. But it is useful to have an action plan and to be aware of what might sabotage it, and also to set yourself boundaries and time limits for the tasks in hand.

◄)) Learn to say no clearly, so that others are in no doubt. Remember, nobody can make you do anything you don't want to. You are master of your own destiny.

SPRING CLEAN YOUR LIFE

As someone who is not naturally domesticated, I have often questioned the pleasure value of cleaning and sorting. But as I have got older and wiser I realise that decluttering and creating clear space really does make me feel better, and in turn my attitude and work are more productive. Cleaning up can hold a great deal of metaphorical meanings for us, especially when we relate it to our personal lives. It does no harm to take a look at the relationships we have both personally and professionally to see if we are hanging on to some that are not good for our health. And if you are finding that the clutter around your home presses down on you and you feel trapped by it, try to find the time to sort it out to give your head, and your house, more space.

Are the people around you 'drains' or 'radiators'? In other words do they take your energy or give theirs? In an ideal situation there should be reciprocity – give and take on both sides – but we probably all have certain people around us who are taking more than they are giving. Identifying these factors can help you to create more assertive relationships.

THE EMOTIONALLY INTELLIGENT VIEWPOINT

An individual's intelligence was once seen only in terms of intellectual or academic abilities. But now there is as much emphasis put on our emotional intelligence – our EQ – as our IQ; in other words, understanding yourself, your needs and emotions, and being able to understand the needs and emotions of others. I believe the way I work with people is from an EQ standpoint, where I encourage them to find their true personal voice, which is a metaphor for their life. By doing so I hope that they will benefit by feeling confident and feeling able to try new paths.

SEE PROBLEMS AS OPPORTUNITIES

Do you see your life as a glass that is half-full or as a glass that is half-empty? I feel blessed to have been born an optimist – with my glass half-full – so I have somehow managed to see the problems I have encountered in my life as opportunities to learn from and grow. If you get into the 'poor me' syndrome – because you see your glass as half-empty – then it is unlikely you will recognise your part in your temporary downfall, because you will be too busy blaming others instead of seeing how you might be part of the problem. Once we acknowledge our responsibility we will have the power to do something about problems we encounter rather than playing the powerless victim.

LIVE FOR TODAY

One very useful thing I learned early on in my quest for self-discovery is that most things in life will seem much more manageable if I take everything one day at a time. Although it is good to review our life, set goals and move forward with a sense of purpose, it is really the thoughts, feelings and actions we take in the *moment* that will create what happens tomorrow. It may sound simplistic, but do try to let go of yesterday – what is done is done, although you can learn from past mistakes, of course. Instead of fearing tomorrow, put your energies into what you can do right now, as what you do now creates the next moment. If you give yourself some time out and do something pleasurable you will have renewed energy and motivation – and it is often in these moments that creative solutions come to us.

SPORT AND WELL-BEING

Studies have shown that exercise is not just important because it improves your health and fitness levels but because it really can make you feel better. Research suggests that people suffering from depression and anxiety feel an improvement in their symptoms through exercise. It is a great mood shifter and energiser on every level, including self-esteem, but it's essential to choose a sport that engages you, otherwise you will be setting yourself up for almost instant failure. Although I love swimming, I will not pretend that I leap out of bed joyously at the prospect of going to the pool, but what I can honestly say is that I have never, ever, in decades of swimming, left the pool feeling worse than when I went in.

Case Study: Upneet

Upneet is a sports performance student and has enjoyed all kinds of sports since childhood, but she particularly enjoys skydiving. She believes that her motivation, self-awareness and confidence have come through her involvement with sport. She says that exercise can help us function better and keep a positive mindset, whatever our stressful life experiences may be:

'I like to think I am a "driver" individual who enjoys taking risks in life and going that extra mile to experience something new and to learn from it. Skydiving is a dangerous pursuit that requires mental toughness and a great amount of self-belief. I always got my drive from sport, but after having jumped out of a plane for the first time, it gave a completely new meaning to the source of my motivation. What started as a desire and attraction to heights became the most inspirational and motivational activity that has helped me develop as an individual ... Skydiving has brought out certain characteristics and qualities in me that I was completely unaware of, and my passion for skydiving has turned me into the person I am today. In practical terms, my ability to lead, pay attention to detail, stay focused under pressure, find confidence and live without fear are some of the abilities I have been able to understand and enhance through my hobby.

'I believe there's a philosophical aspect hidden in extreme sports, which one would need to explore in order to understand. Different things work for different people, and jumping out of planes certainly works for me! I have now done 14 solo skydives and am still a few jumps and mid-air manoeuvres away from qualifying as a fully fledged skydiver. I have had two serious near-death experiences in the same year during my skydiving adventures; I still get nerves while sitting in the door of a plane at 4,000 feet but I have come to realise that the risk is so worth the feeling of achievement I experience each time my feet touch the ground. For me skydiving is a metaphor for living.'

Like Upneet, perhaps we all need to find what it is that truly thrills and motivates us in life. What makes your heart sing? If your life is like one giant jigsaw puzzle but there's a piece missing, look for it to complete the whole picture. If you see life's ups and downs as part of a bigger plan, then nothing will be wasted; even the darkest times ultimately bear fruit and help you to find your own personal voice.

HOW WE LIVE OUR LIVES

The economic crisis has prompted many people to question how they have been living their lives. So much has been imposed on us through the media about celebrity and materialism that I believe it has taken us away from what really matters. Research has shown that there have been more incidents of depression since the Second World War, when there was less materialism and a more prosperous sense of community. The downturn in economic fortunes has also provided us with an opportunity to look at different currencies and to find wealth in other areas of our life apart from materialism.

Homes not houses

Until the meltdown in the housing market there was a great deal of emphasis on house buying, renovation and decoration. There were so many property programmes on television that you couldn't be blamed for feeling a total outcast if you were not in the mortgage market. But now we are in a phase where people are going out less, staying in more and seeing their houses as homes rather than something to do up and sell to the highest bidder. On a personal level, I have lived in different places over the years: in my own house; in rented accommodation; and in a community. I have learned a great deal about myself during that time, and my life has been richer for these varied experiences.

A friend of mine recently told me that since she has lived in cooperative housing she has never felt such inner peace, and it has helped her find her voice in the world. Some years ago she lived in a smart house in a smart road and spent most of her time at work so that she could earn enough money to pay all the extortionate bills. When she lost her business it gave her an opportunity to look at what was working in her life and what was not. Now she has a smaller home, less outgoings and is working fewer hours, she is able to spend more time with her children. Interestingly, her personal crisis enabled her to start a new career coaching young adults, and she says her life has never had so much meaning and she is more contented than she has ever been.

The hidden message in our homes

Our homes can be a symbol of who we are, and often the state of them is an external sign of what is going on inside us. Have you ever considered how fundamentally important your house is to your well-being in terms of your personal and family life, and even your work? Well, Summer Watson, who once worked in marketing and finance and is now a house therapist, has some interesting things to say. (A house therapist means that she works with the 'personality' of a house and how this affects the lives of the people who live there.)

As a house therapist I have seen how important the place we choose to live can be. You *are* where you live! In many ways, when you buy or rent a property you are entering into an intimate relationship with that house. I always say it's a bit like getting married, and it's always interesting to see why a person and a particular house have been attracted to each other.

Over my 15 years of doing this work I have come across houses with all sorts of personalities: divorce houses, sickness houses, wealth houses, poverty houses, single-person houses, loving-couple houses, men-only houses, women-only houses, fertility houses, conflict houses, peaceful houses, jinxed houses and even haunted houses. It's as though each property has, what I call, a 'house-script' and when we walk into that house (or office, come to that) we start to act out whatever is in that script. It is this house-script that will unfold in your life while you are there, and people often see, with hindsight, that their life has taken on a particular direction since moving into that house.

An example of this is when I lodged with a friend after she and her fiancé had split up and she needed somebody to help pay the mortgage once he had gone. She was very intrigued to know what the script of her house was, and how, maybe, it was affecting her life while she was there. When I checked the energy of the house I found that it was strongly female and had the house-script of a 'spinster'.

We decided to check back through the deeds and found that the house had only had two owners since the Second World War – one was a spinster who had lived there all her life with her brother until they were both pensioners, and the previous owner (who had sold the house to my friend and her fiancé) was a widow who lived there by herself. Now that we had checked the history of occupancy we could clearly see that this house did indeed come with a strong 'spinster script'. To me, it is no surprise that my friend had problems with her relationship there and that, eventually, her fiancé left. The script had asserted itself! With hindsight (that wonderful thing!), she was able to see that he wasn't the right man for her anyway and, shortly after selling the house, went to a wonderful new life in Australia.

So, as you can see, the house you choose can have a profound effect on your life – it's not just a pile of bricks and mortar. Perhaps seeing our houses as homes is one of the good things to come out of these credit-crunch times. People are not able to move so easily any more, so perhaps that will make them more conscious about the property they next choose. We are now having to think about the relationship we have with our current home and create more of a 'dialogue' with it. Rather than buying a property and imposing a refurbishment on it to make it more saleable, we should think about how we want to live there and what works for the house and us. I often think that our home is like a large projection screen, and we project our innermost selves out onto it. In a way, our 'voice' is written on the walls. I always try to be respectful of this when I try to help clients make sure the house is reflecting their true voice and the life they are meant to have now.

I was astounded when Summer came to give me a house reading in the home I have lived in with the my three children for the past 12 years. She worked out my personal astrology chart and the time recorded astrologically when we first moved here, and said that this was the perfect house for my writing and creative projects and that it was no accident we had ended up living here.

HOW ANIMALS CAN HELP US TO FIND OUR VOICE

There are different ways to find our inner peace as we work towards improving our self-confidence, and one way is through the stress-releasing relationship we have with the animals we have as pets. As we place more emphasis on homes and our community, we become more aware of how pets might help us. Some American researchers discovered that having a cat can almost halve the risk of having an heart attack, while a study published by Queen's University in Belfast found that dog owners tended to have lower blood pressure and cholesterol levels. This is because animals can help us feel less stressed. Other studies have shown that children with pets have better self-esteem and there are visible benefits for those who have behavioural disorders, such as autism. The list is endless.

Ingrid Rylance is an animal communicator and works with people to create better relationships with their pets.

She believes that animals can help humans in many ways, including confidence-building and raising self-esteem. She says that animals are critical to a human's well-being. There are heroic tales of creatures that have come to the aid of humans: dogs and horses, particularly, have a bond with people and there are many stories about how they have found help for their injured owners. As part of the Pets as Therapy Scheme, dogs and cats are taken into hospitals, care homes, residential and special-needs centres to bring a different kind of healing to the residents. The animals, who are first vetted for their suitability, are stroked and petted by the patients. The scheme has proved successful, with numerous reports of how the animals have helped improve many patients' health.

If pet owners are having problems with their animals, Ingrid can help them by communicating directly with the animal. She also practises distant healing through photographs or using a lock of hair, and by tuning into the animal, emotionally, mentally and spiritually, she can find out exactly what is going on. She said she has been able to resolve all kinds of situations, because the animals have been able to communicate with her and tell her what is wrong; problems have ranged from being unhappy about a name change to a horse's saddle not fitting properly. She says the key issue is that animals live in the present and can help their human owners to do that the same.

I don't know whether animals understand every word, but I feel they understand from a different place; they feel what you are saying rather than understanding every word in the way of speech. This is instinctive to them, for their survival, and their own knowledge. Animals often flee before naturally dangerous situations occur, such as earthquakes, because their instincts somehow warn them. I believe that in some way the instincts of our pets teach us how to be our true selves and how to connect in a more intuitive way. I think this is what we need right now to help us understand each other. Some people find it is easier to communicate with their pet than with another human being.

THE PATH THAT'S RIGHT FOR YOU

It really doesn't matter which road you take to find your personal voice, because just in the same way that each one of us is unique so is the road we choose to find meaning in our lives. If it feels right, go for it, because that means you are in the flow. Once you are in that place there will be no stopping you. Achieving a sense of well-being will produce extraordinary results in both your home and work life.

Children are part of our life's journey, whether we have them ourselves or not, and in the next chapter I look at our experiences and relationships with them and how we can help them to find their own personal voice.

9
Children and Young Adults

P art of our journey to find our own personal voice will involve children. Whether we physically have them or not, the younger generation will have an impact on our life. Our desire to have children, or what happens when we can't have them, and the difficulties we might experience when we do, affects the way we think and feel. They are an integral part of how our lives develop.

But what about the children themselves? How can we help them to find their own personal voices? Being a single parent has been a rewarding, and at times challenging, experience for me, but my main goal has been to help my children find their individual voices. How to balance that freedom of expression with clear boundaries has always been part of an interesting journey for everyone concerned!

In my work I have met adults who have had to deal with all kinds of issues surrounding children, such as their inability to have them, or having children with disability problems, or coping with the loss of a child. I have marvelled at the way these individuals have coped in the face of such difficulties. In this chapter I want to share with you how they have learned through their experiences with children, or without them, and also how adults have helped youngsters to develop and grow, in spite of difficult circumstances or ill health.

THE FERTILITY EXPERT

How does a woman cope if she longs for her own child but can't conceive? If a woman wants to give birth, she is being deprived of a primal experience if she is unable to have a child. How does this affect her ability to find her personal voice? One person who knows both sides of this experience is Melanie, who is a fertility expert and yet has so far been unable to have her own children.

Case Study: Melanie

'The need to find my voice for my own personal journey and for the work I do to help other people has been one of the most important quests I have taken. My partner and I have been trying for a baby for a few years now; we've had our hopes raised and dashed through several miscarriages.

'Through my work as a herbalist and reiki healer I have been lucky to work with some amazing couples who have experienced similar problems to myself. Even though this work is sometimes painful and emotional, it is fundamentally about helping that person to love and respect themself. Unless we can learn to look after ourselves, then true healing can never take place.'

Melanie believes that fertility depends on many factors including physical, emotional and spiritual well-being. She says that some people have long and difficult journeys with fertility, and often find that their lives are profoundly changed because of this.

'I often wonder if fertility issues are merely a catalyst to uncover one's true self. I have witnessed couples become more deeply in love, separate and go their own ways, become great artists, singers and dancers, change their careers, set up their *own businesses, adopt or foster children or go on to give birth to their own children – the possibilities are endless, if you have a willingness to be open for this to happen.*

'In my own personal journey I had been torturing myself by feeling unfulfilled in not being able to carry through a pregnancy, but then I took up dancing and singing – something I had always wanted to do and never had the confidence – now I can do both in front of friends and family. My work, not surprisingly, has taken on a whole new meaning. I am now in the middle of learning about birthing and birth partnering, something which I thought would be too painful to do but now fills me with hope and inspiration.'

For Melanie, being unable to have a child continues to be a difficult journey, but in spite of it, or perhaps because of it, she is discovering a new way to help others when they give birth, allowing her to take part in that special time of hope for a new mother.

UNDERSTANDING DISABILITY

For those fortunate enough to be able to have children, of course, it doesn't necessarily mean that you will not encounter problems. Many parents have to cope with discovering that there's something physically wrong with their child and have to come to terms with the fact that any kind of disability will change the course of that person's and their family's lives forever.

Case Study: Jane

Jane was 23 when her daughter Emily was born in the 1980s, and a week after the birth she was told that Emily had Down's Syndrome:

'I do remember thinking when I returned home with Emily that my life was going to be one long black tunnel and that I would never be able to laugh again. I have been told that parents have two reactions when they are told their child is not normal: either rejection or they are filled with overwhelming love. Fortunately, I felt the latter, although I cannot say I came home from hospital in fighting spirit and never looked back. There were many dark days, and 20 years ago people's attitudes were very different.

'I was fortunate to meet some fantastic parents who were coming to terms with their grief at not having a normal child and not knowing what the outcome would be. There was also some amazing work being done by the Down's Syndrome Association at the time to try to change people's attitude and to foster a much more positive outlook.

'Emily was always treated in the same way as the rest of the family; she had to take her turn and we tried to make sure she had a normal upbringing, and never made her feel she was different. I can also honestly say that having Emily has always brought out the best in people, they have tried to help, been sympathetic as well as inquisitive and responded to Emily in a positive way.'

Jane has had to find her voice as the parent of a child with special needs, and over the years has taken on the medical and educational authorities, even taking them to court, in an attempt to win the best schooling for Emily. She says that in the process she became demonised, but never gave up her fight to be heard and to raise the profile of the needs of children with Down's. Needless to say, life continues to be challenging, as Emily is now in her twenties but has a job and a great degree of independence.

'Emily really enjoys life. She loves music and dancing and has travelled extensively in Europe, and last year went to Dubai and swam with the dolphins. She is an ambassador for Down's

people and gets a lot out of life. The future is a move towards independence; perhaps her own place. She loves family and friends. I am aware that a large number of Down's people get Alzheimer's relatively early in life, so it is important for her to live life to the full now.

'Emily has brought both great joy and sorrow – she has profoundly changed my life and me for the better. She throws herself wholeheartedly into life and cannot bear to miss a thing – and she loves unreservedly. It is a lesson for all of us.'

In these stories we have seen how loss and difficulties have contributed to these individuals finding their voice. It seems that experiencing grief and loss has enabled them to discover a strength and wisdom that perhaps they might otherwise not have known.

COMMUNICATING WITH CHILDREN

Part of the journey we make as children is how we communicate with our parents. If we receive constructive criticism as well as praise there is a good chance we will grow to be rounded adults with healthy self-esteem. It's up to us as parents to send the right messages to help our children respect other people, learn to be caring and responsible, and to build their self-confidence. We do this through clear communication.

When communicating with children you have to be clear about your message and your boundaries, and you also have to think about your audience. Every human being is unique and we have to take into account who we are talking to. Each of your children will respond differently to the way you communicate with them; I found that what might have worked with one of my children was not guaranteed to work with another.

I have noticed over the years that those parents who rely on manuals and guides to raise their infants and children sometimes seem to lose touch with their intuition and innate common sense. My children taught me a great deal from the day they arrived in the world, and some of those lessons included how to relate to each one as an individual, from babyhood through childhood. By the time it came to my third child I was more relaxed and adaptable than I had been with the other two, but I noticed that because she had to fit in with the rest of the family she has always been secure yet independent.

SOME BASIC DOS AND DON'TS

Children and teenagers need to know that you are interested in what they have to say. It is a fundamental need to be heard. Although every child and young adult is different, here are some pointers:

- ◄)) Be careful about the language you use. Never ridicule; for example, don't use: 'You are stupid/lazy/bad.' Instead, try: 'When you did/said that . . . I felt . . .'

- ◄)) Give positive feedback and constructive criticism.

- ◄)) Be aware of your own agenda. If you are tired or stressed about other things, don't take it out on your child. Find the right moment to communicate important points.

- ◄)) Practise what you preach and encourage honesty and open communication – it is better to find out what has happened, however bad, rather than not know at all.

◀)) Communication is vital between parent and child, but remember to use language that the child will understand and relate to.

◀)) Use a calm tone of voice and body language – don't convey mixed messages.

◀)) Make sure you make time for your child and are involved in their life.

◀)) As well as showing interest, don't interrupt them when they are trying to tell you something.

HELPING CHILDREN OVERCOME DIFFICULT CIRCUMSTANCES TO FIND THEIR VOICE

Many children experience a real lack of opportunities and motivation because of difficult situations at home, and it can often be down to a teacher or a mentor to help that young person find their voice and achieve their potential in life.

Ann teaches at a school that serves an area of social and economic deprivation. She believes that poor self-esteem, poverty of aspiration and lack of opportunity limits her students' achievements, but she has also seen kids developing when they are supported and encouraged.

Case Study: Stacey

Ann recalls the great strides that one of her students, Stacey, made with Ann's help:

'Much of my work is concerned with allowing students to realise that they are valued for their own abilities and that their skills are recognised. I worked with a student called Stacey who had been excluded from a previous school because of disruptive and aggressive behaviour. She was not popular with her peers because she intimidated them, and she found it difficult to relate to many of her teachers. We arranged for her to do work experience at a local university, working in the catering department. She loved it! She was very quick to learn the practical skills necessary to survive in a professional kitchen. The staff in the kitchen took her under their wing and they enjoyed being able to pass on their knowledge to a willing student. At the end of the course the university awarded her a special prize and they organised a celebratory lunch for Stacey and the other students who took part. The real benefit for Stacey was not the acquisition of catering skills but the sense of value being placed on her achievements. This gave her the confidence and self-belief to know that she had skills to offer other people and she was valued for being herself. She has now left school and continues to do well in catering. She was recently awarded a prize through her work with the Prince of Wales Trust.'

Stacey found her personal voice through the confidence she gained learning something she loved and working with people who encouraged and supported her. Ann has helped many other disaffected children find their voice through verbal and written communication and seen youngsters overcome seemingly insurmountable problems. She helped one teenage boy to learn to write and this enabled him to go to college and train to be an electrician. He is now running his own business. Ann has also found that some of the most affecting work for her is with students who have no say in their lives and, as a result, are victims of chaotic and poor parenting.

Case Study: Jodie

Anne explains her work with Jodie:

'Jodie lived in a single-parent family with violent older brothers. Her natural father was in prison and her mother had a new partner. Jodie was a very quiet and unremarkable girl. She didn't like being noticed and she found it hard to sustain friendships. She was a talented footballer and she was asked to help with coaching a primary school team. She worked with a local community group to raise funds for girls' football so that the team could have proper kit. As a result of this work she met people who acted as advocates for others, and she started to attend the youth group set up to support young people in the area. Jodie is now a peer counsellor. Not only does she voice the concerns and interests of young people in the community but she also works with individuals at school who need support in coping with their lives. She is an inspirational student who has used her own experience in a powerful way to try to make a difference for other students. Raising self-esteem and giving young people the confidence to take part is the most powerful way to help them overcome their feelings of disaffection.'

What I love about these stories is that they prove how we all have talents, and it is just a question of being to able to discover our abilities. That discovery can be made through the help of a mentoring figure such as a teacher.

GROWING WITH OUR CHILDREN

Teenagers are just starting out on their journey alone; we can help them by trying to understand how difficult it sometimes is for them, and remembering that we were teenagers once. Here are a few thoughts:

🔊 Be there for them. Sometimes, even though our teenage children are living with us, we feel lonely, because their lives are no longer so closely involved with our own. It's an important time in their development, but the more independent they become in some ways the more they need us there in the background. They need to spread their wings but they also need adults to set certain boundaries while allowing them to grow.

🔊 Be approachable. Try to be the kind of listening parent that your children will want to communicate with. Don't believe that by not talking about things they won't be happening; many parents are kept completely in the dark about what their children are doing. If you're an honest and receptive listener it doesn't mean you're condoning what your child is doing, it just means that it's a safe place for them to talk about things that are going on. Being an honest communicator is the best way to help your children, whatever their age.

🔊 See the funny side. Humour has been an essential part of my family's home life. I have found that being able to understand where they are coming from but not trying to be too much a part of it seems to have generally worked for us. I remember my eldest daughter once said to me that she secretly thought I was doing a pretty good job of being her mum but there was no way she was ever going to let on to her friends!

🔊 Keep talking. My bottom line has always been that my children have to be honest with me and to communicate. Lying or blaming is a bigger crime in our house than practically anything else.

🔊 Talk to other parents of teenagers to compare ideas. Bringing up children is mostly about learning as you go along, but it's always helpful to know that other parents are as much in the dark as you are, and together you can decide on strategies that will work well.

The work that teachers and other trained professionals do is essential to help children who are disadvantaged, but adults in other walks of life can also make an important contribution. Many adults who have consciously had to work on finding their own personal voice discover that passing those skills on to younger, less fortunate people is particularly rewarding. Many of us have been lucky enough to be brought up in a family environment with the opportunity to develop our skills and talents, but some young people have not had that benefit and come from a damaged or dysfunctional environment. Sometimes the only chance they get to experience a more 'normal' situation is when they are fostered or adopted, or go for respite care to a family.

HELPING THOSE IN FOSTER CARE

Children can be moved from foster home to foster home and this can have a deep impact. Some foster carers, however, feel their role is to help those children find self-confidence as well as a secure environment and care. Isabella, now a retired foster carer, feels saddened by the way the system moves children from place to place, but she did whatever she could to help those who stayed with her. She feels that children in most circumstances can be helped if people who are responsible for them take the time and trouble to support and encourage them.

Case Study: Isabella

Initially, Isabella wanted to become a foster carer because she cares about people. Also, having been a single parent she felt she had the life experience and understanding to do the job. She wanted to help those children have a better life.

'Over the years I've had children staying for just a few days or up to a year. It seems to me that children are treated like a commodity and moved around randomly. I believe that the children are really affected by this transient world they have to live in. When they are taken away from their parents they feel that loss, but they can then become fond of their carers, so when they are taken away from them as well they feel another loss.

'Fostering gave me the chance to see the good in these children that perhaps other people had stopped seeing. I saw that some of them had been written off by society, but everyone deserves a second chance. I always enjoyed being able to encourage the children in my care. Any interest they showed I tried to encourage and suggest ideas to make it a reality for them.

> *'Nobody should be written off, whatever they have done or whatever their circumstances.*
>
> *'As a former foster carer I always spoke the truth. I think we need to go beyond political correctness and help these children to find their voice and to feel part of society.'*

COPING WITH LOSS

When we see other people coping with what life throws at them *and* succeeding against all odds it can be inspiring and motivating for us. One such woman is Pamela, now in her sixties, who has had to deal with the death of one of her children, a battle against cancer, helping her daughter and grandchildren who were the victims of a violent home life and who now cares for her 85-year-old mother. This is her story:

Case Study: Pamela

Pamela spent two years trying to get a clear diagnosis of her teenage daughter's breathing problems, but her persistence resulted in her being accused of having Munchausen Syndrome (when parents deliberately create an 'illness' in their children so that they can get some attention for themselves). Through sheer persistence, however, the medical authorities finally told her that her daughter had cystic fibrosis – but she had had to travel 500 miles to get the correct diagnosis.

It took years of private tutoring, in between countless hospital admissions, to get her daughter into university, who did enjoy a fairly normal life for a while. She died seven years later.

'I had found my voice through those struggles, but when she died, my voice seemed to be silenced by her death ... I was thrown into a stillness. What did I miss most about her? The sound of her voice. The beauty of that time, though, was that I was still enough to listen to the wisdom of my own true voice. It showed me the way to allow my grief to be present and eventually to transform me. And just in time too, because within six months of my daughter's death I discovered I had breast cancer ... getting through this time has helped me to understand that I can dance with fear and move through it. I found doctors who let me make the health choices I wanted to make, and I got well.'

Now, Pamela has been helping her other daughter and grandchildren flee a violent home. She also looks after her ailing mother.

'These events in my life have helped me to find my voice and I am continuing to find it and trust it.'

We so often hear older people criticising the younger generation or in some ways treating children as though they should be seen and not heard. Yet, so many people who have turned to therapy in adulthood have had to deal with issues of not being heard or speaking their truth – and these problems have invariably started in childhood. So, in this changing world of ours we now have an incredible opportunity to help give children the chance to find their voice. Perhaps instead of blaming young people for the problems in society we need to look at why they sometimes turn to drugs, drink or crime, and how we as adults can help them to express themselves more creatively.

In the final chapter I'll be sharing with you some of the different ways that people have discovered their own voice and how it has led them towards rewarding and satisfying occupations. Each story is individual and inspiring.

10
A Continuing Journey of Discovery

On my personal journey to find more of my voice and to help others find theirs, I have been inspired by countless people who have discovered their own particular ways to speak their personal truth, sometimes through great adversity. I felt this book wouldn't be complete without including the stories of some of those individuals. They come from all walks of life, and have been able to discover more of themselves through their work, creativity or business, in their own unique way. I hope that, like me, you find their experiences to be inspirational and that they will encourage you to find your voice – whatever your situation.

WRITING AS DISCOVERY

Julia Green is a children's writer and course director for an MA in writing, and she says that the students she works with often talk about wanting to 'find their voice' or to reconnect with who they really are.

Case Study: Julia

'Young People often talk about wanting to "find their voice". They seem to be searching for a way to express themselves through their writing, to "say something" important, in a way individual and unique to them. Some have a driving need to be "heard" or to "make their mark".

'For many of our students, the decision to take a year to "write" seems to be a decision about getting closer to themselves: to re-connect with the person they think they really are (creative, imaginative, playful, joyful). For "mature" students, it often means they are deciding to step away from the life they have found themselves in as an adult (lawyer; teacher; computer programmer; theatre director; parent; care worker, whatever).'

Julia's own experience of becoming a published novelist was similar to the people she teaches on her course, when she left the academic world of words to write fiction. For her, that change felt like coming home, and the whole process was one of discovery. Julia believes that writing can truly help an individual find their voice and discover who they are.

MANY 'VOICES' FROM ONE VOICE

For some people the concept of finding their personal voice takes on a different meaning. Linda Newbery is an award-winning novelist and she has talked to me about how important it is for a writer to find a strong voice for each character in the stories they write. This ability comes from the author's own life experience and confidence. A writer is communicating with others through the novels they write, and this can be achieved when an author has found their own voice in life.

Case Study: Linda

'When you begin, you probably try on many different voices, as you might try on fancy-dress costumes. You can't help being influenced by the writers you admire. Having taught A-Level English, I know that many people are uncannily good at imitation; when I set students the task of writing an extra episode of Fools of Fortune *in the style of William Trevor, or of* The Bell Jar *in the style of Sylvia Plath, I was astonished by some of the results. Others in the group, no matter how hard they tried, couldn't get it at all. And it was noticeable that the students who were most successful couldn't analyse what they'd done. Some writing is just infectious.*

'For those clever mimics, though, finding their own voice might be just as difficult as for anyone else. "Voice" is inextricably bound up with viewpoint, period, character, situation, class and upbringing, prejudices, bias and many other factors, which is why it can never be a settled thing, but needs considering for every character and every story. All the choices you make as a writer are bound up with "voice" – and only part of it is concerned with hearing your characters speak.'

Linda says that the two essential things an author needs is structure and voice:

'For instance, one of my novels, Set in Stone, *is set in 1898 and is narrated alternately by my two main characters. The challenge was to create distinctive "voices" for both Charlotte and Samuel, while making both convincing as late Victorians; but once I had a clear sense of both and could move confidently from one to the other, the convolutions of the plot fell into place.'

Linda says that confidence is a large part of producing a convincing 'voice' for each character and that it's crucial that an author believes in his or her creation. Otherwise, readers won't be able to.

POETRY AS COMMUNICATION

It seems in recent years that there has been a resurgence of interest in poetry. Poetry is intended to be spoken and not read, and in that way it is a direct form of communication – and one that many people enjoy. A poet needs to find the confidence to read out their poem to a group, but it can be extremely rewarding to do this before a group of appreciative listeners. Sue Boyle runs a poetry café where people can share their work. This is one of her poems:

The poetry study group
We are all plain Marthas here – not one
has Helen's smooth sweep of jaw, long brow,
the calm gaze of her blameless eyes.
Success has touched none of us;
money has not accrued;
Monday through Saturday we work
and worry cramps our shoulders like a death.
But tonight we have opened up
your poems together
in this quiet room;
razored them for sharing; bent back
the bloomy skin-shapes and revealed
the secret of crimson.
Your poem is a ripe fig.
It has crossed an ocean.
We are preparing, together
to eat life.

Sue believes that sharing a poem seems to bring people together and to break down boundaries. She says a really good poem has the capacity, at least for a while, to create a true community.

Case Study: Sue

'In my little poem I also wanted to catch the way a poem can have secrets, a richness inside itself which it is willing to give up only if you are receptive and open enough to what it wants to say. The act of giving and receiving a poem is a tremendous act of trust.

'When people come together around a poem there is, in my experience, a great delicacy, sensitivity and kindliness – people really are reaching out to hear the voice inside the poem and to let the voice be heard.

'The voice gets stronger when it knows that it has a receptive audience. The listening really is part of the process. When a poem enters the space beyond the poet's self, when it finds room for itself in the shared space which is the public domain, that particular little piece of utterance now has a chance of surviving, and perhaps, if it gets published, if it is good enough, of being able to speak to listeners not yet born.'

THE EXPERIENCES OF CHILDHOOD

I think that often our childhood dreams can become our reality when we recognise their value. Tessa Strickland co-founded the publishing company Barefoot Books for Children and she believes that that vision was born many years before:

Case Study: Tessa

'When I was a child, I loved to write and paint and draw and dance and listen to stories. It takes time to do these things, but the doing of them took me into a space where clock time falls away, and gave me a way of making sense of what was happening around me and to me, and what this all felt like. On the wall of the classroom where I spent my early years, there was a poster that showed lots of different children from other countries. This poster fascinated me: everyone wore strikingly exotic costumes, often with bright colours, and I learnt that they spoke different languages too, and ate different foods, and lived in places that were very different to the part of rural north-east England where I was growing up. I wanted to know how to speak in other languages, and over the years I began to realise that writing and painting, singing and acting, are like languages. So too are more obvious everyday activities like gardening, cooking, farming, furniture making: they all give us ways to express who we are and what we care about. They are the activities that create our culture.'

Tessa says that when she became a parent she started to realise that what happens to us when we are young shapes who we are in ways that we only begin to appreciate much later.

'By my mid-thirties, it was time to re-evaluate my life; to identify what was precious to me and to do what I could to pass it on to my own children, and to other children too. I distilled my list of precious things into a few key words: diversity (in all its forms: ecological, artistic, cultural, linguistic); imagination; interdependence. And I decided that for me the best way to communicate these ideas to children and their parents and educators was through picture books.

*This is how I came to set up Barefoot Books, an independent
publishing company which draws on the art of cultures
all over the world to create picture books. Central to the
business's values is the image of the barefoot child, who is
still free of the kind of cultural conditioning that can over-
value one way of living over another; the child who is still
free to be inventive, resourceful, inquisitive, kind. I believe this
child is alive in all of us, whatever age we are, and that by
looking after our inner child as adults, we become better able
to look after the rich and diverse and remarkable world that
is our shared home.'*

For Tessa, Barefoot Books became a way to express all the
experiences she recalls, right from childhood, and to treasure
that special time that we have as children. When we recognise
that all our experiences are valuable, we can then use them to
enrich our life – and our voice.

THE WRITING ON THE WALL

Creative expression is a central theme to finding one's
voice in life, and for some people drawing and painting is a
replacement for the written word. Mez is a young designer
who has just set up his own company. He believes art has
been the most important form of communication for him
since he discovered drawing at an early age. As a teenager
he found that graffiti gave him a freedom of expression
that he had never found before. Although graffiti is seen as
vandalism in many instances, for others it is seen as an art
form. For Mez, however, even though he broke the law, his
graffiti expressions proved to be a stepping stone:

Case Study: Mez

'School bored me, but when I started to go out with spray cans when I was about 12 it made me feel like a superhero. I went out in the middle of the night with a different alias and with a gang of like-minded people and it was like a step up from army-type games – it was like going on a mission with an end in sight.

'When I started it was along the walls next to a riverbank and by the railway lines. It gave us the privacy to do our artwork without being stopped by the police, yet the next day our "pieces" were visible to hundreds of people on the train. It felt like fame. The whole point of graffiti is to become famous, or infamous, through your work.

'When I ended up in court two years later and got an ASBO it annoyed me at the time because I couldn't believe I had used so much paint, spent so much time doing this work and never really achieved the status I wanted! My graffiti career was cut short because I was arrested.

'But then I was given the time to work on canvases and develop my art. I think all this and my love of art has helped me to discover who I am and to express myself. One reason graffiti helped is because there are no real rules, but there are some unwritten ones. One: you don't copy or "bite" someone else's style; you have to have your own unique style. There is no other art form like this. I found it frustrating at school because I was always being told to copy someone else's style. It is the uniqueness of graffiti that has helped me to develop my own style of art and that is how I have found my voice. I have set up my own art design company and hope to become a successful entrepreneur.'

Being given an ASBO actually helped Mez to explore his artistic 'voice' further so that now he can make a living from his creativity.

GOING WHERE YOUR HEART TAKES YOU

With the popularity of televised talent shows where people can achieve 'instant fame' it is all too easy to see why celebrity status has such a magnetic attraction. But ask anybody in the public eye and they will tell you that it is not always what it seems. Dom Tighe is an actor and a singer who recently made the brave decision to leave the award-winning classical band Blake, because he felt his true voice lay in acting.

Case Study: Dom

'I have often come across this phrase "find your voice" in my life. Most notably was at drama school, where I trained as an actor for three years. In this industry there are two definitions to the phrase "finding my voice". The first is a practical and literal sense of the phrase. I had endless classes about understanding the machine that is the voice. We explored different traits that the human voice could stretch to, including resonance, pitch, singing, accents and how, as an actor, you could apply these "tools" to a character that ultimately aids the telling of a story.

'Secondly, there is the more metaphorical sense of the phrase. In this sense you might refer to it as "finding my purpose, my reason for being" – a sense that still had relevance whilst at drama school, but as I discovered, is something that cannot be taught. You could have the best, most experienced teachers in the world, but when referring to your "voice" in this sense it is a profoundly individual voyage of discovery that you only start to get a better understanding of once you have experienced more of life.

'Something peculiar happened in 2007. Unexpectedly I formed a group called Blake, and within days of meeting one *another ended up with a record deal with Universal Records. I had just been touring the world in two Shakespeare plays, The Taming of the Shrew and Twelfth Night, with the all-male company Propeller and the Old Vic. Suddenly I found myself in a recording studio recording an album with the Royal Philharmonic. As you can imagine, it was an exciting time for me and the other three guys involved. I was having a ball. By default I had ended up in a classical boy band and was travelling the world singing our songs. I had to ask myself how I ended up doing this, having had such a clear focus on what I wanted to do since starting drama school. The advice I received from everyone was, "Don't think about it, just enjoy this once in a lifetime experience!" They were right. When was I ever going to have the chance to do something like this again? So I was now a professional singer."*

Dom says that for a while it didn't matter that he had turned his back on the acting, but then he realised his singing wasn't giving him the same sense of elation that he had enjoyed from acting.

'It wasn't like speaking Shakespeare or playing Chekhov. Beautiful as it is there are only so many emotions that songs like 'Moon River' can present. There was no storytelling involved in the songs I was singing, no emotional journey of a character to discover. It became apparent that dealing with real human emotions and interacting with other actors using speech was, for me, wholly satisfying.

'I felt so strongly that I had lost focus that two years later I decided to leave the group. I was walking away from something really successful but I had "lost my voice".

'"Finding your voice" is an evolving entity; later on I could use acting as a political platform to get a message across. I could be in a film that opens the world's eyes to an issue, but for now acting, or "my voice" is my way of understanding better who I am. It highlights what my strengths and weaknesses are. It

is my way of communicating my thoughts and dealing with emotions. A filter for my life. Am I any good at it? You'd have to ask the audience.'

Dom's training in acting taught him to use his physical voice and to find his personal voice. Once we have decided to take this journey to find our personal voice, we owe it to ourselves to act on what we have learned to develop it further and live our lives with the confidence to express ourselves fully.

A LIFELONG JOURNEY

The arts can have a profound effect on our lives, whatever age we are, and many people as they get older are regular theatregoers or would like to become more involved in drama. David Manzi-Fé is an actor, storyteller and director who has recently turned his attentions to working with the elderly, helping them to find their voice. David grew up near Stratford-upon-Avon in the 1950s and was brought up reading, listening and watching Shakespeare's plays. He later discovered acting and stage-managing, mime and street theatre.

Case Study: David

'Later, I had fun learning, or should I say discovering, storytelling. So my dreams and imagination began to work, and through this my true voice began to emerge. It took time, but storytelling really helped with my own individuation.

'At about the same time some friends and I started to put on amateur Shakespeare productions. I realised that for me my "voice" was coming through as a director/producer.'

And when many people who turn 60 might be thinking about taking life a little easier as they head towards retirement, David went on a year-long full-time director's course, which led to him setting up a small touring company, which he says helped his confidence and finding his voice on a different level.

'Now I am really interested in using theatre in a social context rather than just as "entertainment". I have two projects starting up, the first is to use Forum Theatre with older people, like myself – people who are entering into old age and the journeying that that entails. And the second is to create an amateur theatre company using people over 60 who would like to play with the myths and delicious journeys held within Shakespeare.'

David realised how vital his work in dramatic productions had been to the development of his own personal voice, and how he had found that his own journey continued way past his fifties. It's heartening to know that whatever our age we can enjoy the benefits we will gain when we find our own voice and continue to grow.

HELPING OTHERS BE HEARD THROUGH POLITICS

There is no doubt that British politics will be changed for ever in the wake of the expenses scandal. Even before this debacle many people viewed politicians with mistrust and from now on it will matter more than ever that politicians stay true to their word. One person who is longing for that opportunity is Clive Allen who is hoping to be elected as an MP.

Case Study: Clive

'I am one of those with a fairly rare view that political ambition almost always starts with good intentions. I want to become politician "to make a difference" or to "change the world".

'So why go into politics . . . ? Money? Power? Fame? A desire to change things for the better? Perhaps a combination of all four?

'Could it be that the same type of person is attracted to the similar careers/vocations: politics, the Church, the law or acting? Consider this: each of them requires similar characteristics – apparent self-confidence, the desire for public recognition, a degree of acting ability, an ability to persuade and an overwhelming sense that your view is the right one.'

Clive says that it's for these reasons he has passionately followed politics for years and stood for Parliament twice, and intends to stand again.

'As for all the cynicism about politicians, I still believe that you can make a real difference by actually trying to do something. The number of doors I have knocked on on a cold, wet evening to ask for the support of the voters only to receive the refrain "you lot are all the same", "you won't change anything" – the apathy party wins again. I am now driven partly to prove the cynics wrong. Even in small ways, a politician can help to make people's lives a little better if they choose to do so.

'What motivates me to run for politics? It would be true to say that I enjoy the ability to stand in front of an audience, to influence, to persuade to affirm, even to entertain. But I also look at the number of people who find themselves up "against the system" or trying to improve their lot. Having an advocate, a supporter, a fighter who helps them represent their interests, who helps them to have their voice heard, is a truly humbling and rewarding experience.

> *'So what would I like to achieve? One of the most powerful rules that I try to run my life by is that my aim in life should be to help make the world a better place when I leave it than it was when I joined it. Politics just happens to be my chosen path to help me try to achieve that ambition.'*

For Clive, helping others to be heard, and wanting to make a worthwhile contribution to society to make the world a better place, is all part of his own personal journey to find his own voice.

OUR PAST CAN HELP OTHERS

Many people find their voice through helping others, and perhaps some of the most appreciated occupations are those in health care. But what drives someone to work with other people in a professional capacity? Rebecca believes that she found her voice as a doctor because of her own personal experiences.

Case Study: Rebecca

'I was just 16 when my first baby was born. I was treated so badly that I decided then to be an obstetrician, but there was no support or educational opportunities available then for unmarried mothers – I had been expelled from school as a "bad example". At the same time, I nursed my mum who was dying from a brain tumour. She died six weeks after my seventeenth birthday and ten days after I got married. My second son was born when I was 18 and I ended up doing night shifts as an auxiliary nurse and eventually had to get credits from the Open University so that I could do my degree and then train as a doctor.

'I started my joint honours degree when my oldest son was 10. During my interview for medical school I was asked questions that wouldn't have been allowed under today's discrimination laws, such as how I planned to cope with studying and children, and what my husband thought about my plans. I remember telling them that I believed that if a person was determined enough then they could achieve anything ... I got my degree and started medical school when I was 29.

'I eventually qualified and was working some pretty gruelling hours as a doctor when I received a call at work from a solicitor in my home town. He had traced me to ask me if I'd stand bail for and offer pre-trial accommodation to my father. He'd been charged with the indecent assault of his second wife's 16-year-old niece. I felt sick as I began to think about him, and for the first time remembered odd incidents from my own childhood that at the time I'd pushed away as inappropriate touching. Then I realised I'd left my 13-year-old sister alone at home with him when I got married when Mum died. I'd moved away, neither of us had telephones, I'd not been in touch at all. My sister had gone to live with Dad's parents. I phoned her and found that for all those years my sister had known things about our father that I'd completely forgotten until then. I don't know what our grandparents knew. My sister couldn't, and still can't, talk about it – but she had always made sure that she didn't leave her daughters alone with him. He went to prison for three years and was put on the sex-offenders register when he was released.

'Since that trauma I have had to cope with my son's alcoholism, but he is in good recovery and our relationship is better now. I'd always felt guilty that perhaps when I was a medical student and at work I'd not been around to help him when he needed it. But he has assured us this is not the case. But the experience has helped me find my voice working with the homeless and addiction issues.'

Rebecca has experienced so much in her life, but she says these experiences have contributed to her work as a doctor. She felt drawn to train in the medical profession, even though it was difficult for her in many ways – and this shows how committed she is to helping others and to using her experiences to find her voice.

FINDING A VOICE THROUGH CARING

Sarah started her career in the travel industry and, as well as bringing up four sons, has been a childminder and then ran a pub. Her later work as a carer in a residential home for the elderly, however, has been one of the most fulfilling experiences of her life.

Case Study: Sarah

'I enjoyed the very first day. The elderly have so much to give in terms of wisdom and advice. They have seen it all.

'I discovered that I had a skill for helping and caring for people – a skill for communicating and understanding their needs. I felt I had an empathy with them and could appreciate all that will have happened to them and all that they have been through in their lives. They weren't just some demented old fools lost to the world and being a nuisance. This could be me in 40 years' time. Maybe some of the problems I have faced have made me appreciate the hardships they have been through. Something had brought me to this point in my life and at this juncture I felt able to work with these elderly people and to learn more about them and their needs and illnesses and how to help them in the last days, months and years of their lives.'

Sarah says that the saddest part of her job is caring for the dying:

'The first time I saw someone die was quite profound. Unfortunately, this person was in considerable distress and I recall being with her and stroking her forehead and saying that she was not alone and that we were with her, then the light went from her eyes and she was gone. It is deeply moving when you witness a life ending; I can only say that I was honoured to have been able to be with her and whisper those words in her ear. This wonderful lady, whose life had ended so painfully and whose mind had been so twisted by dementia, was a shadow of her former self. Since then I have witnessed others dying. If I can, I always make a point of whispering that all is well and that they are not alone, touching them and stroking their arms for comfort. It never gets any easier; each person is an individual with different circumstances.

'Another aspect of the job is dealing with dementia. It is not straightforward and no one person has the same symptoms. And yes, it is an illness. Not every old person has dementia. People like to joke about having Alzheimer's or dementia and yet you do not joke about having cancer. Dealing with it requires skill and patience.

'I feel I have found my voice doing this work. I know I am good at it and don't mind saying it, but I get so much pleasure from it as well. The staff with whom I work are equally caring and are a good set of people whose company I enjoy. There is a huge amount of laughter and humour at the things that some of the residents do and say. We are not laughing at them but with them. We are dealing with such highs and lows of emotion that we have to adopt a "gallows humour" that may seem hard at times. If we did not laugh, then the enormity of it all would get to us and we would never stop crying. In truth we all care too much.'

Sarah's skill in caring for the elderly, the respect she holds for them, and the understanding she has for them is heartwarming reading. Having had many life experiences before she worked with the elderly has helped Sarah to understand their contribution to all of our lives. It has enriched her own journey and she is able to enrich theirs as they end their lives.

EMBRACING INDIVIDUALITY

In the world of business and finance some individuals have been finding their voice through the career of their choice or by helping organisations to find theirs. Interestingly, any time I have met an accountant they always seem to apologise for their career choice and make the inevitable joke about being 'a boring old accountant', which is not necessarily what they are at all. In fact, some people who are blessed with great creativity and humour choose to work in the financial world, and are not only successful but also enjoy what they do.

Dave Ingle is co-director of his own accountancy firm and, as his story proves, has discovered how important it is to do what you want in life and to find your voice. Reassuringly, not being good at maths at school doesn't seem to have got in his way!

Case Study: David

David's first job was at the age of 17, which came as a result of thumbing through the phone book – it was a temporary position as a filing clerk for the Inland Revenue. Later he became a chartered tax adviser.

'I confess I sat my O-level maths three times in all, once at school and twice at college in evening classes. Failed, miserably –

ungraded on all three occasions. Not bad for an accountant. Anyway, one thing I was good at was chatting, because this is the bit I enjoy. In fact my current business partner calls me a chartered chatter and I can't argue with him.

'It's been 18 years since I set up my own firm, and I am happy with it, it's not exciting or racy but it earns a good crust, I can chat all day and do as I please within reason. I guess I could have gone further with the other firms I worked for and become successful, but I enjoy this.

'All through my working life I have done other things to make ends meet or to give me some "pocket money" like fixing cars and motorbikes. Even now I am still at it – currently building some flats. I guess I like getting my hands dirty and having the comfort of an office job. I think we all have a level that we operate within that we feel comfortable with. Some have a higher level and are prepared to take risks, and some are not. The real entrepreneurs have no ceiling and no fear of failing.

'For me I don't worry about what people think of me, I used to but not any more. Back then I had no confidence. Now I just don't care. People take me for what I am. My firm gets most of its work by word of mouth, and potential clients are sometimes warned. "Ahh you're the accountant that rolls up on a motorbike."

'"Yep that's me. It used to be a bicycle, but I have moved on!"

I don't even own a suit, I don't need to stand on ceremony for anyone, if you don't like it then get another accountant; I know my job, my confidence is high.'

David is a real individual and likes to use that to his advantage by working as an accountant who has an air of relaxed confidence. He uses his past experience of coaching individuals to make sure he communicates with his clients in a way that is clear and encouraging – and he helps many to overcome their worries about their finances.

'My years of working as an employee of an organisation and as a coach helping individuals and groups within business has shown me how important it is for a company to find its voice. If you have a toxic workplace then it is very difficult for the employees to find a clear and constructive way of communicating.'

INDIVIDUALS' VOICES MAKE A STRONGER WHOLE

Bryce Taylor is an author and co-director of the Oasis School of Human Relations, which has helped over 80 business schools and global organisations interested in developing new approaches to the way employees and managers in companies and organisations work together.

Case Study: Bryce

'There's a difference between making a noise and finding a voice. The problem in most organisations is that there are plenty of people making a noise but about very different things. So, any hope of hearing one voice is highly unrealistic.

'An organisation doesn't have a single voice – it may have a strong identity, a brand that is easily recognised; but organisations don't usually have a single voice.

'Uniformity of sound is not the same thing as sweetness of harmony, and many organisations attempt to impose some version of uniformity on their contributors in the hope that it will bring about a similar conformity of action – and we know only too well it doesn't. But organisations do need to find some form of unity; some form of bringing together the different contributions of all those involved in ways that respect and appreciate the differences that are required to make the whole thing work.

'There's a great deal of talk about team playing. A better

analogy to my mind is the choir. An organisation is a lot like a choir in some respects. There is a lot of practising to "sound" right to get the "right" contributions in the right order to hear the separate and distinct notes that individuals and sub-groups bring to make up the whole: just as there is the need to bring all those contributions in to some sort of alignment in creating the effective organisational effort.

'Alignment is my magic word because it recognises that people don't have to do the same things, but that whatever they do needs to "fit" somehow in relation to the overall effort, and they need to know what that is and what value it adds.'

For Bryce, each individual voice is essential for a successful organisation, but everyone must work together to make the whole venture work well. He believes that it's important for each person to find their own voice, because this will, in turn, benefit the company as a whole.

GAINING RESPECT FOR BEING HONEST

Mark Line is one of the UK's leading authorities in corporate and social responsibility and helps companies to become more socially and environmentally responsible. He's not afraid to speak up and be honest about those issues that he feels need addressing in an organisation, and has become admired and respected for his candour.

Case Study: Mark

'We approached this new market from a deep understanding of the science behind the environmental issues and social performance. We quickly found that our work was respected for

*its integrity. We gained a reputation for "telling it how it is" –
and also being willing to help solve real problems, rather than
just spouting theory.'*

Mark says his company Two Tomorrows found its voice
when they realised that clients respected being challenged by
a 'critical friend', and that that way of working continues to be
one of their key roles; for example:

*'We were actively encouraged to develop an "independent
assurance" service – where we form an opinion on how a
company "is faring" on its sustainability practices and to decide
whether what they say about themselves holds water. So our
"voice" developed through the public opinion statements that
we wrote. We found that "telling it how it is" was respected by
those clients that were serious about their programmes.'*

Mark says that to keep their reputation they not only have
to know what they're talking about but also be willing to
speak out when necessary.

*'This might mean publicly challenging a claim that cannot
be substantiated, or even pointing out when a company is
underselling its story, or missing an opportunity. We also found
our voice through building relationships with key people
within client organisations. We came to realise the ironic truth:
companies are made up of people whose personal values may
not directly align with those of their employers.*

*'I have found that speaking from the heart and talking
common sense is respected by the people with whom I interact.
More often than not, I will be invited into meetings specifically
because people know that I will tell it how it is – and as time
has gone on I have become increasingly confident in speaking
out when the real issue is being avoided.*

*'So how does this kind of honesty translate to the individual
in business? I am a big advocate of being yourself. The only
person you can sell is you and your uniqueness, so why try to*

be anyone else? It is important to capitalise on your strengths rather than struggling to better your weaknesses. A company's success is dependent on its players and a team is made up of individuals with different strengths.

'Some of the most successful people in business, and entrepreneurs, are those individuals who did not necessarily do well at school, and these days it is more important than ever to try and find the work you love to do. As any successful business person will tell you, there are times they have had to "fake it to make it" because they do not necessarily feel as confident as they appear, and very often the most talented person in business has not started off with the supposedly right credentials.'

Mark puts a lot of emphasis on being yourself and selling the qualities you have as a person, not trying to be anyone else. Your strengths are what are important, not your weaknesses. It makes inspiring reading and encouragement for anyone who is still hesitant about speaking truthfully.

CONFIDENCE THAT SELLS ITSELF

Riley Sims left school at 18, with no qualifications, a fear of authority and a painfully shy personality, but became a very successful businessman because he was able to capitalise on his own unique talents.

Case Study: Riley

'I quickly realised that if I was to get on, I needed to do something about my shyness and my introvert character, so I became a salesman for an internationally renowned

photocopier company. I discovered that my shyness was, in fact, an attribute rather than an obstacle. I found that I listened intently to what people were saying. I also found that I could create an empathy with customers and I could create long-lasting and trusting business relationships. I rarely used closed questions, requiring yes or no answers, as I found this built obstacles to full and frank discussions. Open questions, allowing people to express opinions and feelings, helped me to understand that person, what motivated them and to use that valuable information for our mutual benefit. I was very successful, not only in a selling role, but also as a sales team manager by applying the same techniques. Never aggressive but able to communicate effectively in a tone and at a level where clients and staff alike never felt threatened.'

Riley's career developed and he worked all over the world and overcame potential communication barriers with his clients:

'I learned, when talking to people whose first language is not English, that I needed to keep my speech very simple, and not to use the full beauty and subtlety of the English language with its nuances, double meanings and use of metaphors. I found this worked like magic.

'In developing my own businesses, I like to think I not only got the best out of my employees but also that I helped them develop their own careers through the art of communication. I tried never to talk down to anyone. I always tried to communicate at their level in terms that they would understand immediately and be at their ease in conversation. I am now very comfortable in talking to anyone at all, and to this day I still apply the principles learnt through my experiences.'

Riley explains that his clients often bemoan the fact that they are good at their core business but find the selling part difficult. In actual fact, he finds that most people are good at communicating about their own business when speaking to him, and so he encourages them to use those same communication skills to promote their business to potential clients.

'My response is always, "You are communicating brilliantly with me, and this means that you can communicate brilliantly with anyone." The art of selling is to communicate; listen, learn, know your client and never use closed questions unless you need to draw a meeting to a close. Talk at their level and they will not feel threatened. You will create empathy. That empathy will lead to them buying you – not just what you are offering.'

These are encouraging words from someone who has found the road to success by being himself and a great communicator.

All the stories in this chapter sum up the message of this book: have the confidence and courage to be yourself. Finding more of your voice in any personal or professional situation is the key to success. The great thing is that you don't have to try to be anybody else – being *you* is your unique selling point.

As we've seen in some of the stories above, finding more of our voice is a lifetime's journey and one that can give us so much pleasure. I do hope this book has encouraged you to continue with your journey – and while you discover what makes your voice unique, remember: it's about progress, not perfection!

Index